CHOCOLATE CHIP COOKIE SCHOOL

by Susie Wyshak and Friends

CHOCOLATE CHIP
COOKIE
School
Detective in Training

www.ChocolateChipCookieSchool.com

First Printing, 2015 (Rev. 1)
ISBN: 978-0-9967017-0-9

Suggested for ages 8-12

JNF001000	JUVENILE NONFICTION / Activity Books
JNF025080	JUVENILE NONFICTION / History / Exploration & Discovery
JNF010000	JUVENILE NONFICTION / Business & Economics
JNF014000	JUVENILE NONFICTION / Cooking & Food

Ordering and Contact Information:

Quantity sales: Special discounts are available on quantity purchases by schools, home schools, corporations, associations, and others.

Orders by U.S. trade bookstores and wholesalers as well as corrections and suggestions, please contact:
susie@chocolatechipcookieschool.com or 510.269.7794. Or visit www.ChocolateChipCookieSchool.com for more information.

MANY FUN WAYS TO USE THIS BOOK

Printables and worksheets are available to download at ChocolateChipCookieSchool.com

Designed for kids 8+, this book is full amazing stories, fun facts, and inspiring inventions. The many exercises will inspire critical thinking through cookies. Rather than being just an awesome treat, cookies become a learning tool!

Ideas for Teaching With This Book

The many topics make the book ideal for home room units, homeschools, after school programs and unschooling situations—or even a fun vacation project.

1. Read the book for fun and general education, without doing the cookie project.

2. Project-based learning (in Part 2): After reading Part 1, embark on Part 2, planning a bake sale or business individually or in groups.

3. Several-week unit: Study each ingredient per session, then undertake the project in Part 2.

How Chocolate Chip Cookie Detectives will put their school knowledge to work:

English - Learn the stories, see how legends and idioms came from foods we eat every day.

Science - Decipher how ingredients transform into the perfect cookie.

Math - Accurately measure, buy ingredients and calculate prices.

Food systems and shopping skills - Get thinking about where food comes from and how to make it, from techniques to tools.

Geography and history - Trace the cookie ingredients' journey through time and space.

Social science - Learn the stories and decide if things could have happened in some other way.

Character Skills - Readers will appreciate how collaboration, curiosity, calculated risks and perseverance lead to innovation, fun and success in the real world!

CONTENTS

Part 1: Learn Cookie History

Part 2: Make Cookie History

Worksheets

More Information

PART 1:
LEARN COOKIE HISTORY

When you make OR eat chocolate chip cookies you are connected to a world of people and places.

+100 YEARS AGO
The Cookie Dark Ages;
No cookies with chocolate chips existed.

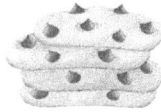

AROUND 1930
A lucky someone ate the **first chocolate chip cookie!**

TODAY
Millions of people **around the world** enjoy billions of chocolate chip cookies.

FUTURE
Future cookie fans will seek out new cookies... maybe yours?

THE FIRST TIME SOMEONE ATE A CHOCOLATE CHIP COOKIE

Imagine it's the 1930s, when the world was in "The Great Depression."

People are struggling to find work and feed their families. Jobs are hard to find. Food is scarce. Still, people need to travel from place to place. In Whitman, Massachusetts, there is a road stop with cheap, delicious meals. It's called the **Toll House Inn.**

Imagine being there…

Imagine you are a diner at the Inn. You've eaten a nice, filling meal. Then you see this delicious cookie, with little bits of chocolate. You smell, then taste the very first chocolate chip cookie ever made. Since that first bite, the world has not been the same.

Where did that amazing, new cookie come from?
Only a Cookie Detective can crack this case!

INVENTION LEGENDS

We don't know for sure how the Toll House® Chocolate Chip Cookie came to be!

Some stories say chocolate accidentally jiggled into the cookie mixer then broke into chips. Other stories say Ruth Graves Wakefield, who owned the Toll House Inn with her husband, used "chips" on purpose as a substitute for nuts. Or maybe she just wanted to create something different for her guests.

Was it an accident?

Or an invention?

Analyze the legends! Exercise on page 70.

How can this be? Isn't it easy to know historic facts?

Well, times were different before the Internet. Even telephone calls outside of local areas were really expensive. Stories took longer to get around. When a story spreads person by person, by word-of-mouth, the more a story tends to change.

WHAT GOES INTO A COOKIE?
TAKE A CLOSE LOOK

Read through each ingredient and each step of the classic Toll House® Chocolate Chip Cookie recipe.

How many foods and tools you see?

ORIGINAL TOLL HOUSE
CHOCOLATE CHIP COOKIE RECIPE

Ingredients

2 1/4 cups of all-purpose flour

1 teaspoon baking soda

1 teaspoon salt

1 cup (2 sticks) butter, softened

3/4 cup granulated sugar

3/4 cup packed brown sugar

1 teaspoon vanilla extract

2 large eggs

2 cups (12 oz. pkg) chocolate chips

1 cup chopped nuts (optional)

Steps

1. Preheat oven to 375 degrees.

2. Combine flour, baking soda and salt in a small bowl.

3. Beat butter, granulated sugar, brown sugar and vanilla extract in a large mixer bowl until creamy.

4. Add eggs, one at a time, beating well after each addition. Gradually beat in flour mixture.

5. Stir in chocolate chips and nuts.

6. Drop by rounded tablespoons onto ungreased baking sheets.

7. Bake for 9 to 11 minutes or until golden brown. Cool on baking sheets for 2 minutes; remove to wire racks to cool completely.

Dying to get started baking? Flip to page 58.

THE COOKIE JOURNEYED
THROUGH THOUSANDS OF YEARS AND MILES

Making cookies is easy today. But a lot had to happen for the right ingredients and tools to come together at the right time and at the right place, at the Toll House Inn.

In fact, the chocolate chip cookie's invention was only possible due to lots of hard work, daring, creativity and many happy accidents over the years. This map shows a tiny bit of cookie history.

The ingredients come together at the Toll House Inn.

You will draw this map for real as part of your Cookie Detective challenges!

THOUSANDS OF YEARS AGO
People discovered fire, farming, preserving and many cookie ingredients.

1400s-1800s
Explorers discovered, traded, or stole ingredients to make more food for less money.

1700s-1800s
The Industrial Revolution began a frenzy of food production inventions. Food that once was expensive and rare became common.

EARLY 1900s
Standardized recipes, measuring tools and electric baking equipment simplify baking.

PREPARE YOUR
COOKIE DETECTIVE TOOLS

Prepare to tap into your natural powers as a Cookie Detective! You already have the skills to connect the dots between the past and present of America's favorite cookie.

Your Cookie Detective thinking cap and attention to facts and clues, help you connect the crumbs!

Your spirit of happiness helps you celebrate as you learn and use your critical thinking.

Creativity helps you see the world in new ways and invent new ideas.

A sense of humor and risk taking let you know there are no "mistakes," only "experiments."

Collaboration and **teamwork** help you solve big problems and make work like play.

Curiosity leads you to try new new things, ask **what** and think critically about **why** and **how!**

SUGAR HISTORY AND MYSTERIES

The journey of sugar to the Toll House Inn began thousands of years ago in New Guinea, an island in the South Pacific where the people grew reed-like sugarcane as crops.

Sugar was once rare, which made it an unusual treat for royalty. For common people like us, sugar was a valuable medicine and spice, not a cheap sweetener. Back then, honey sweetened most desserts and drinks.

Ah, life is sweet!

TIMELINE:

1513: Spanish explorer Juan Ponce de León landed on a lush coast. He named it La Florida, or "flowery land." Florida's tropical climate was perfect for growing the sugarcane plants he brought from the Caribbean.

1600s-1700s: Europeans fell in love with sugar and sweet desserts. Money-hungry Dutch, French, Spanish, and British colonialists raced to grow the sugar industry. To make the most money, they needed cheap or free labor. Colonists enslaved Africans, transporting them on dirty, crowded ships. Many slaves got sick and died. Poor people from other countries, and even children, were lured to work in sugarcane-growing areas as cheap labor.

1751: Jesuit priests brought the first sugarcane plants into the Louisiana Territory, in the United States. Plantation owners worked the slaves hard, in pursuit of riches.

1760 TO THE EARLY 1800s: The Industrial Revolution was a time of modernization and invention. New canals, roads and railways made it possible to transport sugarcane and sugar to new lands worldwide. The industry grew.

1835: The first Hawaiian sugarcane plantations cropped up on the island of Kauai. During the Civil War, the northern states would not buy sugar from slave-owning southerners. This helped Hawaii's sugar industry big time. Over 50,000 Chinese came to work the fields.

1843: Norbert Rillieux invented a brilliant Sugar Evaporation System...a really BIG deal (see p. 10).

LATE 1800s: After slavery was abolished, sugar cane plantation owners lured millions of Chinese, Japanese, Korean and Filipinos with promises of a good life. Working conditions were usually horrible. Workers who asked for more money often got a big fat nothing, then were replaced with cheaper workers!

1959: Hawaii became a U.S. state, and the tourism industry became more profitable than sugarcane.

TODAY: Most sugar is produced in Brazil, India, China, Mexico, Australia, Thailand and Pakistan. In the U.S., sugarcane is grown in Florida, Hawaii, Louisiana and Texas. Sugar from beets is a huge industry, too.

Making Sugar Out of Cane

In ancient times, people made sugar by grinding and pounding plant stalks. The sun evaporated the water. This left just sugar crystals!

3 Phases of Cane Sugar

- **Unrefined** = raw sugar
- **Refined** = white sugar
- **Refined sugar coated with molasses** = brown sugar

The Big Sugar Refining Invention

Norbert Rillieux was the son of a rich Louisiana plantation owner. He was well-educated and became an engineer and inventor. He designed a machine in the 1830s which began the sugar-refining process.

The Rillieux Apparatus solved big problems of processing sugarcane and beets into sugar: It cut down the amount of sugar wasted in the refining process. It made the process safer. Slaves no longer had to transfer boiling sugar juice between kettles with ladles. Phew!

The resulting white sugar is also called granulated sugar. Because each grain is a _____

Did you know?

Sugar is the world's largest crop!

Manufacturers produce 1.7 billion tons of sugar a year.

N. Rillieux,
Vacuum Pan,
Nº 3,237.
Patented Aug. 26, 1843.

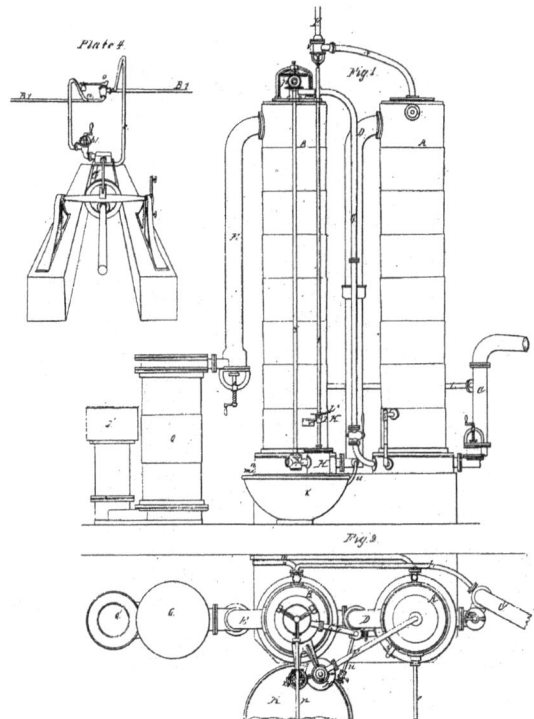

Original patent drawing of the apparatus of Norbert Rillieux from 1843

Cookie Detective Query

Slavery made it cheap to produce sugar. What other ways could sugar have been made cheaply, while also treating workers well?

_____

_____

_____

_____

_____

_____

_____

Thank That Sugar For Your Cookies!

Sugar plays a big role in how your cookies turn out. Baking is chemistry, and sugar seriously transforms with heat (see page 63).

- Sugar tenderizes the dough by shortening the flour's gluten strands. Sugar browns the cookies, and brown sugar makes cookies even browner!
- Sugar is a moisturizer, which helps keep the cookie fresh after baking.
- Creaming sugar and eggs with butter creates air cells. This helps the cookies rise so they are light and fluffy.

Did you know?

Cookies don't always need granulated sugar.

Lots of sweeteners can make cookies sweet. You can use dried fruits, like dates, instead of sugar. That's because those fruits are full of fructose, the natural sugar found in fruits.

Of course, when you change one ingredient, other parts of the recipe need to be adjusted. Why is that?

How to Spot Sugar

Sugar is made of a substance called sucrose. All ingredients ending with "-ose" are sugars. Fructose is sugar from fruit. Maltose comes from starchy seeds like barley. Do you know where we find lactose?

If sugar were grown more widely in the U.S., how would that impact the sugarcane market in the U.S. and around the world?

_____

_____

_____

_____

_____

Selling sugar

- o What topics does this 1912 sugar ad talk about that you don't see in ads or TV commercials nowadays?
- o Why do you suppose those topics were important back in 1912?

_____

_____

_____

_____

_____

_____

_____

_____

_____

2 lbs.
NET WEIGHT

CRYSTAL
Domino

REG US PAT OFF

Extra Fine
**GRANULATED
SUGAR**

MANUFACTURED BY
THE AMERICAN SUGAR
REFINING COMPANY

This is the Package

After the sugar has been safeguarded in our refineries by exacting laboratory tests to insure its absolute purity, we want to be *certain* of its reaching you as pure as it leaves the refineries so automatic machinery receives, weighs and packs the sugar in dust-tight, germ-proof packages. No hand touches the product from refinery to user.

In germ-proof packages only
No flies—no dust

Sold by grocers in 2 and 5 pound
Sealed packages. Guaranteed weight

THE AMERICAN SUGAR
REFINING COMPANY
Address—New York City

Sugar Speak

What do these idioms mean?

Try using the phrases in conversation. How do you feel when you say or hear them?

- o Hey sweetie!
- o You're so sweet!
- o Sweet talking me
- o Sweet tooth
- o Sweeten the pot
- o Don't sugar coat it!
- o Thanks, Honey!

What other sayings or idioms relate to sugar and sweetness?

_____

_____

_____

_____

_____

_____

EGG HISTORY AND MYSTERIES

The BIG question is: Which came first, the chicken or the egg? Of course, Ruth Graves Wakefield did not need to know the answer to this question to invent the cookie. But she did need easy access to eggs!

Thousands of years ago, people figured out that eggs were a good source of food. Raiding a nest and cooking over a fire must have been easier than hunting!

TIMELINE

BEFORE 10,000 BC: People in China were raising chickens, according to fossil records.

2500s BC: Chickens migrated over trade routes to ancient Egypt. Royal tomb walls had drawings of chickens. People hung eggs in the temples to pray for good crops. That's some good luck charm!

1493: Columbus brought chickens on his second trip to America, the New World. The many English colonists must have been very happy to get this familiar food from back home in their new country!

1911: Joseph Coyle designed and patented a carton with compartments for each egg. He got this idea while trying to solve a dispute between a farmer and hotel owner about broken eggs!

THE BIG BREAKTHROUGH: Now eggs could be transported from farms to the city without breaking.

TODAY: The U.S. produces many millions of eggs per year. Many farms raise hens in large factories, with birds terribly crowded together. Many food companies have begun using eggs only from "cage-free" hens...NOT "factory farmed" hens. The future looks happier for our chickens and for our health!

Try invention, not contention

What good things did Joseph Coyle get out of inventing the egg carton instead of getting in a fight?

_____

_____

_____

_____

_____

_____

Thank That Little Egg For Your Cookies!

- Eggs provide structure. Egg protein binds ingredients. Without eggs, your cookie really would crumble.
- The fat in egg yolks works as a team with butter. Fats shorten the gluten strands in the flour. This also tenderizes the cookie.
- A beaten egg holds lots of air. Air pockets are important for baking! When the cookies are in the oven, the trapped air expands and helps the cookies rise.
- Eggs add moisture to recipes. They are over 70% water!
- Eggs add better flavor to the batter. The yolks brown easily in the oven and add to the cookie's deliciousness.

Egg-citing Science

Describe what a chocolate chip cookie might look, taste and feel like without the eggs.

_____

_____

_____

_____

_____

_____

_____

Meet some modern-day food inventors with a big idea...

Delicious chocolate chip cookie dough that doesn't have eggs OR butter?! In 2014, a company called Hampton Creek® created a dough that would make vegetarian cookie lovers very happy.

They discovered plant-based ingredients that could substitute for eggs. Their recipe tastes a lot like the original Toll House® Chocolate Chip Cookie.

What are some big benefits of eggless cookies?

* Remember this eggs-ample when planning your own cookie company!

Packaging Egg-cercise

In 1913, Stuart Ellis designed an eggs-by-mail carton, after cities banned urban chicken farming. Some cartons were metal. Many were (and are) made of cardboard. **Which material do you think is better? Why?**

_____

_____

_____

_____

_____

_____

Eggs in cartons sometimes break. What might solve this problem?

_____

_____

_____

_____

Jan. 31, 1933. J. L. COYLE 1,895,974
EGG CARTON
Filed Oct. 21, 1927 2 Sheets—Sheet 2

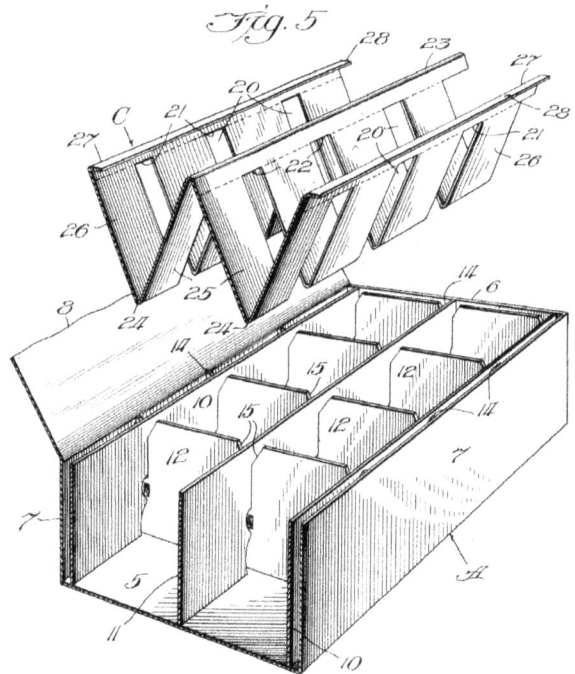

Egg carton patent from 1933

The Price of Eggs

☐ When the supply of eggs goes down, do prices go up or down?

☐ What happens when prices go too high?

Find some other examples of products that are on sale. Why do you suppose the store or website marks down the prices of some things and not others?

Did you know?

What's better than an A+? An AA!

The best grade an egg can get is AA. This means they are really fresh! As eggs age, their grade goes down to A or B. The white becomes watery, the yolk is less firm and they may sink in water. Fresh eggs float!

Egg Speak

What do these phrases mean?

Try using them in a conversation!

- ☐ Don't put all your eggs in one basket!
- ☐ He's a good egg.
- ☐ She has egg on her face.
- ☐ Pecking order
- ☐ Chicken-and-egg situation
- ☐ She's no Spring chicken!

How to Annoy Your Friends

Is there **no end** to all the possible egg puns? Apparently not! See what words that start with "ex" you can change to eggs instead.

_____

_____

_____

_____

Cookie Detective Query

Chickens normally only lay eggs in the warm season, unless they are on farms that have warming lights or warmer climates. The Christian Easter holiday and Jewish Seder celebrate the return of spring with eggs!

Do chickens in warmer climates lay eggs all year long? Why or why not? Find out!

_____

_____

_____

_____

VANILLA HISTORY AND MYSTERIES

Imagine a world without vanilla. Now imagine: one kid made vanilla possible!

TIMELINE

MID-1400s TO 1500: The Aztecs discovered vanilla (a pod from the Vanilla orchid flower) when they conquered the Totonac Indians in Mexico.

1520: The Spanish conquistador Hernan Cortés arrived in Mexico and conquered the Aztec Indians — a big time for conquering! Montezuma, the defeated Emperor of the Aztecs, greeted Cortés with a drink called "Chocolatl," made of ground corn, cocoa beans, honey and vanilla.

1602: After many years of the noble and rich enjoying chocolate (thanks to Cortez), a new flavor was born: Hugh Morgan, aide to Queen Elizabeth I, tried vanilla as a flavoring by itself for the first time.

1789: Thomas Jefferson had a lot of firsts. He had the first vanilla in the U.S., which he ordered after tasting it in France. Philadelphia soon got famous for fine vanilla ice cream. Even George Washington was a huge fan!

1730s-1800s: Aspiring vanilla growers stole plants from Mexico, hoping to plant it widely and get rich. But it just didn't grow in other tropical countries. Rumors spread that Aztec King Montezuma had put a curse on the plants. What do you think of that?

Thank That Vanilla For Your Cookies

Vanilla adds a nice flavor to chocolate chip cookies. Without it, cookies are downright boring!

There's pretty much no better promotion than the President giving a thumbs up! ♥

President Reagan was known for his love of licorice Jelly Belly® jelly beans. President Obama fell in love with Fran's Chocolates caramels.

Both of these candy companies did very well, having Presidents as big fans.

Why did vanilla grow in Mexico and not other tropical countries?

Answer: The Melipona bee, only found in Mexico, would pollinate the flowers.

Meet Our Vanilla Hero!

IN 1841, at the age of 12, a former slave named Edmond Albius tried pollinating flowers by hand using a little stick. It worked!

Thanks to Albius, botanists, who are plant experts, successfully planted vanilla in tropical countries like Tahiti, Indonesia and Madagascar. The world supply grew. Vanilla became cheaper (just as sugar did). Sadly, Albius did not benefit from his discovery— which **we** still benefit from to this day.

1874: Scientists created a cheap "artificial vanilla" called vanillin, made from pine trees. Nowadays, vanillin is made from wood pulp left over from paper making!

I'm just not into it!

What skills helped young Albius make this discovery and make sure the right people knew about it?

_____

_____

_____

_____

_____

_____

_____

Cookie Detective Query

- ☐ How did vanilla finally spread to become affordable for us to buy?
- ☐ Why is it still pretty expensive? Why is vanillin cheaper?
- ☐ If you were trying to help the vanilla industry and workers, how could you help?

Hint!

_____

_____

_____

_____

_____

_____

_____

_____

_____

_____

Roadmap for aspiring vanilla tycoons

First plant: Plant 25° north or south of the Equator in an area that has both shade and sun. The elevation should be Sea level - about 2000 feet. Pollinate the flowers by hand.

Harvest and cure the vanilla beans: The green beans, basically pods, dry in the sun by day. Then they sweat in a box at night—for 3 to 6 months. Each country uses a slightly different curing process, which leads to unique vanilla flavors.

Make vanilla extract: Soak the cured, brown leathery pods in an alcohol, like vodka or bourbon for a month or longer.

There's a lot more to building a vanilla empire. Research what else you would need to do if this sounds like the perfect career for you.

It's not easy being a vanilla farmer...

Each vanilla flower opens for only **ONE** day during the season. If it's not pollinated on that day, no pod will be produced! Taking a day off during vanilla season is not an option.

271 done. Only 853 to go...today!

Baking Tip

Even though vanilla adds a nice flavor to your cookies, they will bake fine without it. To make up for the lost flavor, add a small amount of orange, cinnamon or other flavor.

BUTTER HISTORY AND MYSTERIES

For thousands of years butter was yet another rare food enjoyed mostly by the rich and royal. Inventions made during the Industrial Revolution, starting around 1760, changed this. Finally we could make and store butter in large quantities — making it affordable to the masses.

TIMELINE

2,500s BC: The first written reference to butter was a drawing on a limestone tablet showing how butter was made.

1305 AD: Back then, butter was very salty, which preserved the butter for long storage. One recipe called for 1 pound of salt per 10 pounds of butter. (Imagine how salty that is!)

1662: The English passed a law to have standards for making butter, to avoid sickness…and death.

1800: American engineer Thomas Moore packed butter in a metal container that sat on ice in a wood box. Sound like a refrigerator?

1848: The first butter factory was built in New York. Farmers brought and sold milk to the factory. (Before that, dairy farmers sold butter directly to local stores.)

1907: A grocery manager had the idea to cut butter in ¼ pound sticks, for customers who couldn't afford a pound.

1912: Butter companies advertised their new, convenient wrapping and ¼ pound stick sizes.

1924: Machines for wrapping butter in wax-coated paper and cartons hit the market. No more wooden boxes!

TODAY: The U.S. grade of butter (A or B) is determined by first the flavor and then the body, color, and salt content.

What is butter anyway?

In 1923, the U.S. officially defined butter as "a food product made exclusively from milk or cream, or both, with or without common salt, and with or without additional coloring matter, and containing not less than 80% by weight of milk fat." In case anyone asks, now you know!

Then there are butter substitutes!

When you've got something delicious and expensive like butter, people try to find cheap substitutes— especially in war time. In 1869, a French chemist patented margarine, a spread that is now made mainly of vegetable oil and water. Why did he create it? To enter a contest that **Emperor Napoleon III** held to invent a cheap butter substitute.

Next time you bake or fry Try COTTOLENE

Wherever you now use butter or lard in shortening or frying, just try COTTOLENE, the original and best vegetable-oil cooking fat; you'll be delighted with the results.

COTTOLENE makes cakes even lighter, and finer in texture, than when butter is used—and not one in a thousand can taste the slightest difference. In piecrust, doughnuts, and for all frying, COTTOLENE gives better results than lard, and is very much more wholesome.

COTTOLENE costs only about half as much as butter and there is a still further saving in the fact that one-third less COTTOLENE is required; a pound of COTTOLENE will go as far as a pound and a half of either butter or lard.

Try COTTOLENE in one of your favorite recipes; one test will convince that COTTOLENE is "equal to butter, better than lard, more economical than either."

Made by
THE N.K. FAIRBANK COMPANY

The Amazing Wax Paper

That waxed wrapper on butter helps:

1. Preserve quality and flavor

2. Keep out undesirable smells

3. Protect the butter shape and texture

4. Stay sanitary and clean

5. Reduce moisture loss

6. Make handling more convenient

7. Guard against rancidity (or, going bad)

8. Identify the brand and other information

What else do you notice about butter wrappers?

Fascinating Fat Fact

Experts continue to debate if butter or margarine is better (or worse) for you. The important thing for your heart health is to read the label on margarine packages. Avoid any that has trans fats or hydrogenated oil. These oils can lead to clogging of your arteries. Yes, it is as bad as it sounds.

This 1-pound butter slab is a lot harder to use than butter cut into sticks!

- Coconut or other oils can work as a butter substitute in some recipes.
- For lower-fat version of cookies, you can substitute part of the butter with applesauce.

Always remember, changing ingredients means you have to change the recipe!

Butter Idioms

What do these buttery sayings mean?
Find out, then try using them in real life!

- ☐ "Butter up" your teacher
- ☐ "Bread and butter of a company"
- ☐ Want your bread buttered on both sides

Old-Time Butter Making: Churn, Churn, Churn!

In the old days, butter was a rare treat that was very difficult to make.

You churn until you feel like your arms will fall off, and a little while later, the cream turns into butter!

At-Home Butter Making: Shake, Shake, Shake!

Do-it-yourself (DIY) butter is easy! Put very cold heavy cream in a cold jar, put the top on, and shake, shake shake until it turns into butter! Keep your butter refrigerated, and stir in salt if you like.

SHAKE!

In real life, your butter will look more like a clumpy lump. but it sure will taste good!

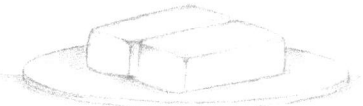

Thank That Butter For Your Cookies!

- When butter creams with sugar and eggs in cookie dough, air pockets form, adding to chewy softness!
- Butter has some vitamin A, E and K. No, it is not a substitute for your daily vegetables. Nice thought!
- Butter adds flavor to any baked good.
- Butter and sugar lead to cookies browning, which is called the Maillard reaction. (How would you like a chemical reaction named after you!?)

FLOUR HISTORY AND MYSTERIES

For as long as people have farmed, they have ground plants into meal and flour using whatever tools they had to simplify the process. (These ancient Egyptians would have loved flour mills!)

TIMELINE

25 BC: An ancient Roman author, Vitruvius, described a watermill with a paddlewheel and millstones. This ancient technology ground grains for many centuries.

1200 AD: Wind mills became popular in Europe and began to power grain mills.

1777: Wheat was first planted in the United States as a hobby crop.

1790: Henry Wood began importing European flour to Boston for bakers in the United States.

1878: A horrific disaster took place in a Minnesota mill. The wheat had passed through the millstone yet the stone kept grinding. Friction ignited a spark. BOOM! Flour dust exploded, killing 22 people and destroying several nearby mills.

1879: The first steam-powered mill went into operation in London, England.

1896: The company Wood founded was re-named King Arthur Flour® and began turning U.S.-grown wheat into flour. You'll still find this flour at the store!

TODAY: Wheat grows in about 42 U.S. states, and ¾ of U.S. grain-based foods eaten are made from wheat flour — pizza dough, bread, crackers and of course cookies!

Thank That Flour For Your Cookies!

- Flour contains gluten proteins that trap carbon dioxide and help cookies rise. (Gluten-free flours can work just as well, too!)
- Flour holds the other ingredients together.
- Flour gives cookies that chewy softness.

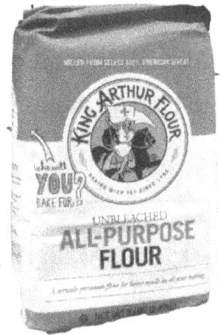

Some say "Every cloud has a silver lining!" Meaning, something good often comes from something bad.

The Great Mill Disaster of 1878 led to safety reforms for workers and for factory operations.

What's the "silver lining" in this story?

_____

_____

_____

_____

This ad appeared in a cookbook. What year is this cookbook from?

Hint: Look at the flour timeline!

Floury Language

It's amazing how some ancient phrases stay alive. Learn these phrases and try them in a sentence.

- ☐ Grist for the mill
- ☐ Back to the old grind
- ☐ Run of the mill
- ☐ Milling around
- ☐ Nose to the grindstone

So Many Flours!

Flour is mostly made from wheat, but it can be ground, or milled, from any of these foods:

- ☐ Acorns
- ☐ Bananas
- ☐ Almonds
- ☐ Rice
- ☐ Chestnuts
- ☐ Coconuts
- ☐ Chick peas
- ☐ Peanuts
- ☐ Peas
- ☐ Potatoes
- ☐ Rye
- ☐ Quinoa
- ☐ Soybeans

Discuss: Which of these flours have you had? Which do you want to try?

Like this ad shows, wheat flours can vary depending on:

- Where the wheat grew?
- When it grew (winter or summer)?
- The type of wheat?
- How it is processed?

King Arthur Flour

MADE FROM THE CHOICEST of SELECTED SPRING WHEAT & Guaranteed to be Unbleached

KING ARTHUR
MINNESOTA

Introduced over twelve years ago, it has held its position as the *Highest Grade* of Flour ever produced

Sands, Taylor & Wood Co.
Boston and Providence

Cookie Detective Query

Do some research on two types of non-wheat flours. Which are gluten free? Decide if they would work well in cookies. (You'll soon learn more about cookie chemistry!)

_____

_____

_____

_____

_____

_____

_____

_____

SALT HISTORY AND MYSTERIES

Salt comes from the sea...

Sea salt is harvested from sea water, which is then evaporated with the sun or other heat sources.

...and from the earth!

Rock salt is mined from the ground using water then evaporated or heated.

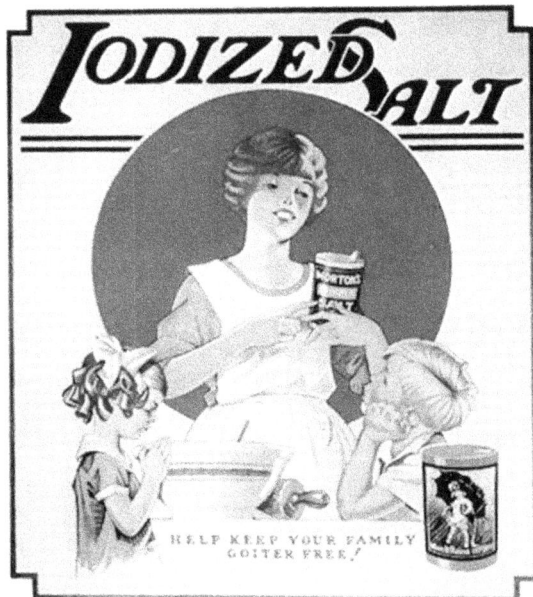

IODIZED SALT

HELP KEEP YOUR FAMILY
GOITER FREE!

In 1924 Morton introduced iodized salt
to help prevent simple goiter.
As significant as that was, if it were the
only thing Morton had done for salt,
it's not likely they would have stayed
America's salt favorite for 50 years.
No salt salts like Morton Salt salts.

MORTON
SALT

Cookies as Medicine?

This 1920s Morton® salt ad talks about the benefits of iodine, a mineral they added to the salt, for our health. What do you think of food that includes added vitamins and minerals?

Here is a brief peek into salt's amazing history and importance in our lives. It may be hard to believe, but people have gone to war over salt!

TIMELINE

3,000 BC: Salt was used for healing wounds and preserving foods, especially meat from hunts.

2,000 BC: "Salt roads" were used to transport salt to places that didn't have any. Hebrews, Greeks, Romans, and many other civilizations depended on salt! They even traded slaves for salt.

1286: Salt was so valuable in France they passed a tax on it to raise money.

1700s: Every year in England, 10,000 people were arrested for smuggling salt, and people could make good livings by mining salt or drying sea salt.

WAR OF 1812: Soldiers were paid with salt (a SALary), as the government couldn't afford to pay them with money...and salt was as useful as money!

1924: Much like vitamins in flour, Morton began producing iodized table salt.

Thank That Salt For Your Cookies!

- Salt strengthens the gluten from the flour.
- It offsets the sweet to make you crave just one more bite!

Salt Talk

Every culture has salt legends, stories and idioms. Learn what these popular sayings mean. Try using them with your friends!

- ☐ Take it with a grain of salt.
- ☐ Back to the salt mines!
- ☐ Salt of the earth
- ☐ Rub salt in a wound
- ☐ Worth his salt
- ☐ Know the work-related word we use today that comes from "salarium?"

Quick: Salt or Money?

Salt is a big part of how our civilization spread around the globe. Some of the largest, oldest cities sprung up and grew because of salt mining. What's the big deal? Salt preserves food. Without salt, and before refrigeration, people had to rely on what they could find or catch. They had to eat their catch quickly before it would spoil!.

Which of the following is NOT true:

1. There are 14,000 uses for salt, including in cooking, industrial and medicine.

2. Some cultures believe salt has magical powers.

3. Salt served as money at various times and places.

4. Wars have been fought over salt.

5. The famous Italian city Venice got rich from salt.

6. China is the world's biggest salt producer.

7. Offering bread and salt to visitors is, in many cultures, a traditional sign of hospitality.

8. It's healthy to eat lots of salt daily.

9. We all need to eat salt to survive.

Answer: 8. Too much salt is really really bad for our hearts and overall health!

Cookie Detective Query

Research the different kinds of salts you can buy today. What's the difference between the flavors and textures? How does the texture vary depending on where the salt comes from?

_____

_____

_____

_____

Given salt's history and uses, is it the most important ingredient you've learned about? Why or why not?

_____

_____

_____

BAKING SODA HISTORY & MYSTERIES

If you think it's cool how heat turns ingredients into cookies, wait until you learn about baking soda. (It's the perfect Science Fair ingredient!)

TIMELINE

THOUSANDS OF YEARS AGO: Ancient Egyptians used early forms of baking soda in their paint for hieroglyphics and even cosmetics.

1791: A French chemist and surgeon started producing baking soda (soda ash).

1846: Austin Church and John Dwight created the first bicarbonate of soda in a New England village. It would soon become packaged as baking soda under the ARM & HAMMER™ brand.

1946: The first trona mine shaft was excavated in Wyoming.

TODAY: Baking soda is used in a variety of ways all over the world. The ARM & HAMMER box highlights what some Cookie Detectives may consider the most important use of baking soda.

Soda Science

Baking soda begins with trona. Trona is a natural mineral that is chemically known as sodium sesquicarbonate. (Say that fast 3 times!) Trona gets refined into soda ash which is used to make glass, paper products, laundry detergents AND baking soda.

Also known as sodium bicarbonate, baking soda's chemical formula is $NaHCO_3$, meaning it's made of the following elements:

- 1 sodium atom (Na)
- 1 hydrogen atom (H)
- 1 carbon atom (C)
- 3 oxygen atoms (O3)

(No, you don't need to know this to make great cookies or run a cookie business.)

Thank That Soda For Your Cookies!

That little cardboard box full of chalky white powder holds the power to puff up your cookies. Without it: flat and hard cookies are the end-result.

Here's how baking soda works:

Baking soda + moisture + an acid produces a chemical reaction. Carbon dioxide bubbles form and make the cookies rise.

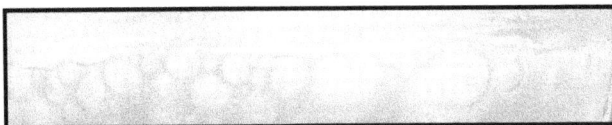

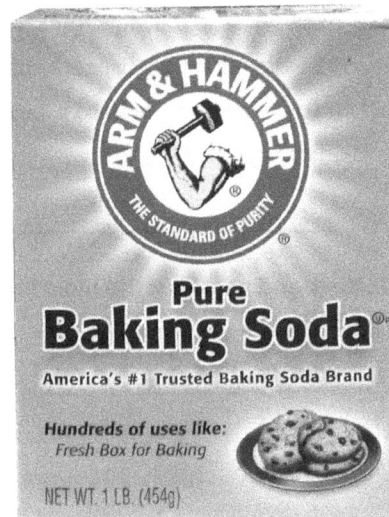

Pure **Baking Soda**®

America's #1 Trusted Baking Soda Brand

Hundreds of uses like:
Fresh Box for Baking

NET WT. 1 LB. (454g)

Amazing Baking Soda

Baking soda is one of the most fun, versatile minerals you may ever encounter. Seriously!

Here are just a few ways you can use baking soda:

- ☐ Cooking and baking (of course!)
- ☐ To put out grease fires, like when frying
- ☐ Reduce stomach indigestion and heartburn
- ☐ Relieve swelling from insect bites and stings
- ☐ Keeping refrigerators un-smelly
- ☐ Cleaning stink out of carpets
- ☐ Whiten teeth (Check out the toothpaste aisle!)
- ☐ Deodorant (Ditto on the deodorant aisle.)
- ☐ Remove rust
- ☐ Clean surfaces
- ☐ Keep swimming pools and spas at the right pH level

Simple Experiments

Log your results for your baking soda explorations below. Remember, if it doesn't come out how you expected, try again. Trial and error produced the very first cookie, after all!

1. Compare baked goods made with baking soda and without.

2. Clean a cookie tray or cooking pan with regular cleanser then compare it to cleaning with baking soda.

3. Mix baking soda with clear, distilled vinegar and what do you get?

A super fun, fizzy concoction that bleaches and cleans like the strongest detergent! If you've got tiles and an old toothbrush, make the mixture, dip the toothbrush in and scrub away.

Baking Soda Experiment Log Book - Let your imagination run wild!

CHOCOLATE HISTORY & MYSTERIES

Can you imagine a world without chocolate? It is yet another food with a wild history...

TIMELINE

1500 BC TO 1500 AD: Olmecs, Mayans, Aztecs and other people of South America, Central America and Mexico grew cacao. They traded, celebrated and made drinks from cocoa beans.

1500s: Columbus and Cortez brought cocoa beans to Spain. No one got what all the excitement was about. Not until the late 1500s did cocoa start to catch on.

EARLY 1600s: Love of chocolate spread to Italy and France.

1739: Benjamin Franklin sold American-made chocolate in his Philadelphia print shop.

1773: More than 320 tons of cocoa beans were imported to the U.S. for drinking chocolate in cafes and to give soldiers energy (just one of Benjamin Franklin's strokes of brilliance).

1785: Thomas Jefferson stated that drinking chocolate would be the #1 hot beverage in the U.S. That was about 75 years before people began eating chocolate!

1828: Coenraad Van Houten, a Dutch chemist, invented a cocoa press that removed 2/3 of the cocoa butter from the crushed cocoa beans. He crushed the resulting chocolate mass into a fine powder—yes, cocoa powder!

1847: Fry's chocolate in Britain made the first bar of chocolate made for eating (rather than for drinking). They used cocoa powder, sugar and cocoa butter. It was edible but very bitter.

1850s-1860s: Etienne Guittard (from France) and Domenico Ghirardelli (from Italy) began making chocolate in San Francisco during the Gold Rush. The people in California had new wealth and a taste for sweets. It was the perfect place to set up shop!

1875: Daniel Peter and Henri Nestlé produced the first milk chocolate.

1879: Rudolph Lindt invented conching (see next page). Legends say he left the grinding machine on by accident, which led to a very smooth chocolate mixture!

1897: Consumers in the U.S. were eating 26 million pounds of chocolate per year.

1900: Hershey began to focus on chocolate, inventing Kisses in 1907.

EARLY 1930s: A cookie with chocolate chipped from a Nestlé® bar is tasted for the first time!

1940s: Some really big things happened ... and you'll be learning all about the chocolate chip in just a few pages. Sit tight!

TODAY: Over 3 million tons of cocoa are produced every year by family farms.

Which of these chocolate makers' names do you recognize? Highlight the names you've heard before.

Hint: You'll see some at the drugstore or market!

Imagine being Etienne Guittard, who founded Guittard Chocolate in 1869 in San Francisco.

Back then, his chocolate factory was in downtown San Francisco, a port town where you now find mostly office buildings. Imagine the time and effort to ship all the ingredients from tropical countries!

How is chocolate made?

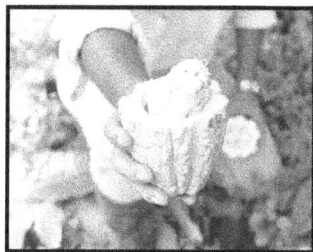

1. Chocolate starts with this football-shaped cacao pod that grows on the side of trees.

2. Workers remove cocoa beans from the pod.

3. Cocoa beans go through a process of heat and drying after which they are shelled and roasted to develop chocolate flavor then ground into bits, called nibs.

4. The cocoa nibs and sugar grind together (also with milk, for milk chocolate) in a conching machine. During 24-72 hours, the mix goes from powder to a warm, wet paste as cocoa butter comes out. More time means smaller particles and smoother chocolate.

Thanks to Guittard® Chocolate for sharing these photos of cocoa bean harvesting and processing.

Cookie Detective Query

The first chips were semi-sweet. Research and write down the many chip flavors available to cookie bakers today.

_____
_____
_____
_____
_____
_____
_____
_____

Why do you suppose most chocolate chips are shaped like Hershey Kisses?

_____
_____
_____
_____

Thank Those Chips For Your Cookies!

Without them, you wouldn't have chocolate chip cookies!

What other foods come from grinding seeds, nuts or beans into a spread or butter?

ON TO BAKING TOOL HISTORY
SPOT THE INVENTIONS!

List all tools used for baking that are missing from this picture.

Hint: You saw them on the recipe, page 6.

Cookie Detective Query

IMAGINE BAKING WITHOUT...

...ELECTRIC APPLIANCES! At home we can use a mixing spoon, and maybe we could use the sun to bake cookies. But doesn't electricity make all the difference?

The Invention of Mixers

In the early 1900s, Hobart Manufacturing started selling large commercial mixers for professional bakers like Ruth Graves Wakefield. This same company created a big mixer for the home in 1919. It's called the KitchenAid™.

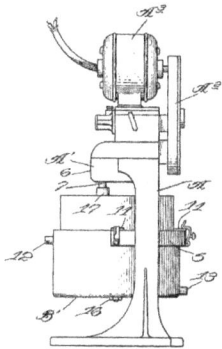

Inventors file patents on designs like these. Then they own the rights to this design. If anyone else wants to use this design, they need to pay the inventors.

Every day, people just like you continue to improve equipment design, making it more functional and user-friendly!

Modern Ovens

This oven was a modern innovation at one time!

Still, bakers probably had quite a bit more trouble getting the same results with each cookie batch than we do with modern ovens. Read what the ad has to say.

Cookie Detective Query

Think of 3 kitchen inventions you are very grateful for. How do they help you?

The invention:

1. _____

2. _____

3. _____

Why it rocks:

_____

_____

_____

A TRULY AMAZING INVENTION
THAT SEEMS SOOOO OBVIOUS NOW!

Here's how people explained their recipes in the old days: "You take a pinch of flour and a cup of sugar." Those cups were any old cup you had at home.

Before 1900, or so, there were no standard ways to measure ingredients. Every time someone said "cup," that cup might have been big...or tiny. Cookbooks used vague measurements such as: Use a ball of butter "the size of a walnut" or "the size of an egg."

Cookie Detective Query

What's the flaw in using eggs and walnuts to measure ingredients?

Imagine if Ruth Graves Wakefield hadn't precisely measured her ingredients. Would her cookie recipe have become famous? Why or why not?

_____

_____

_____

_____

_____

_____

_____

Cookery, 14.
Cookies, Almond, 608.
   Boston, 606.
   Chocolate, 608.
   Chocolate Fruit, 609.
   Cocoanut Cream, 606.
   Cream, 605.
   German Chocolate, 609.
   Ginger Snaps, 602.
   Hermits, 605.
   Imperial, 605.
   Jelly Jumbles, 605.
   Molasses, 602.
   Molasses, Soft, 602.
   Molasses, Sour Cream, 60
   Nut, 608.
   Oatmeal, 604.
   Oatmeal, Nut, 604.
   Peanut, 607.

Quiz: What's incredibly disturbing about this picture of the Fannie Farmer 1923 cookie recipe index?

Answer: No chocolate chip cookies!

Fannie Farmer's 1923 cookbook recipe index

STANDARD MEASURING TOOLS LEAD TO
STANDARD RECIPES

What makes cookies or breads different from each other? A lot of things!

Each recipe changes depending on a few factors:

- The **ingredients** used
- The **quantities** of each ingredient
- How the ingredients are **prepared** (chopped, softened, ground)
- **Utensils and equipment** used
- The **order** that you mix the ingredients
- The **time** to prepare or bake
- Any **heat or cold** that changes the ingredients

When you're cooking foods like steak or an egg scramble, it's OK to change time, measurements and even the recipe, but baking in an oven is much more of an exact science!

Thank Fannie Farmer For Recipes!

Fannie Farmer not only invented standard measuring tools for baking, she wrote **The Boston Cooking-School Cook Book** in 1896. With her book, home cooks could easily reproduce the recipes, thanks to the standard measuring spoons and cups.—that Fannie Farmer invented!

Ever since then, every cookbook and every recipe developer has followed the recipe format Fannie invented. Before her work, it would have been really hard (maybe impossible!) for the same recipe to spread.

Her cookbook has sold more than 3 million copies!

What if we all used the same-sized cup!?

Born in Boston in 1857, Fannie Farmer was known as "the mother of level measurements". She noticed a need for standard measuring tools for wet and dry ingredients. She took action and invented a system and tools we still use today!

The Turning Point for Cooks

Manufacturing of measuring spoons and cups grew in the early 1900s. Soon you could buy those measuring tools at grocery stores and general stores.

Now everyone had the same definition of a teaspoon, a tablespoon and a cup. This meant recipes like the chocolate chip cookie could be shared and spread—quickly!

measuring cup

measuring spoons

MAP YOUR FINDINGS
-OFFICIAL COOKIE DETECTIVE REPORT-

Use what you've learned to map the entire, amazing journey the ingredients and baking tools took before landing at the Toll House Inn in Massachusetts.*

You may want to start by listing the countries where cookie ingredients came from. Oh yes, the map will get very messy. It's hard to fit thousands of years and lines on one map, That's yet another reason to appreciate the cookie and all the great food we get to eat!

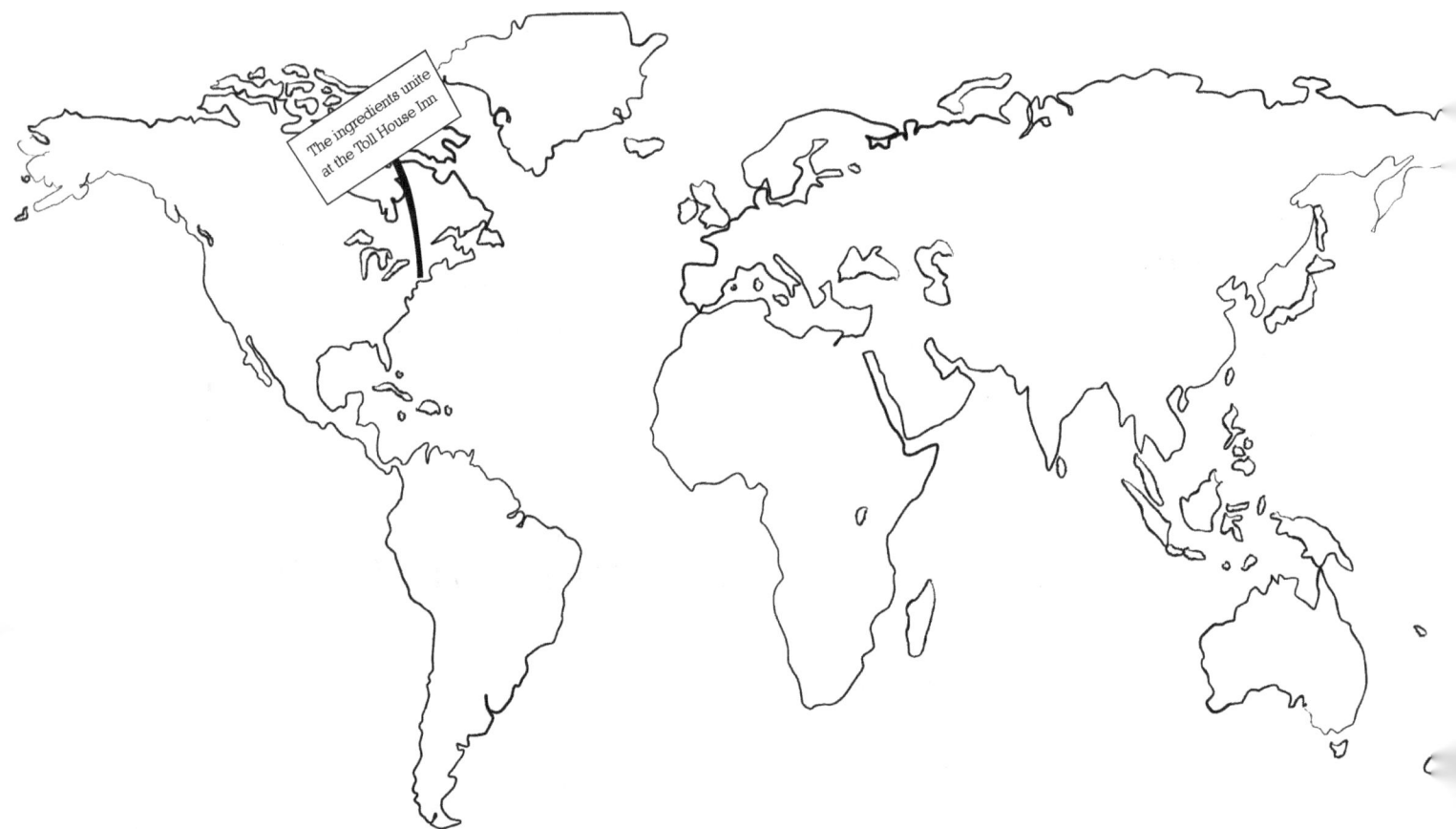

The ingredients unite at the Toll House Inn

*Don't want to write in the book? Download a printable map at ChocolateChipCookieSchool.com.

AFTER THAT FIRST COOKIE
AT TOLL HOUSE INN

News about this new cookie spread like dough in a hot oven!

Guests who ate at the Toll House Inn told their friends. Radio show hosts around the country raved about the cookie and the recipe. Newspapers printed the recipe. Home bakers loved it—they could now easily learn to make the ''Chocolate Crunch Cookies'' from Ruth Wakefield's 1938 edition of her ''Tried and True'' cookbook.

DEAR MOM THE BOYS WILL MAKE YOU AN HONORARY GENERAL IF YOU'LL JUST SEND US MORE TOLLHOUSE COOKIES

Cookie ad in World War II.

Cookie Detective Query

How would you go about telling friends about an exciting new food?

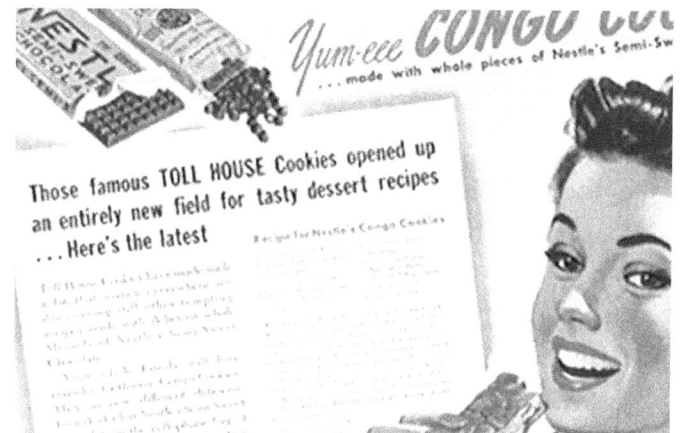

_____

_____

_____

_____

_____

_____

m-m-Everybody's making TOLL HOUSE COOKIES—

SURPRISE

NESTLE'S SEMI-SWEET CHOC

Yum-eee CONGO CO
...made with whole pieces of Nestle's Semi-Sw

Those famous TOLL HOUSE Cookies opened up an entirely new field for tasty dessert recipes ...Here's the latest

...A BIG CHOCOLATE DEAL MADE THE COOKIE A
REALLY BIG DEAL!

What in the world??

Sales of the Nestlé semi-sweet chocolate bar skyrocketed in New England, as more and more people heard about the recipe.

Nestlé connected the dots and met with Ruth Wakefield, the cookie's inventor. (Imagine their curiosity about a baker and business owner who made their chocolate so popular!)

The Opportunity of a Lifetime

On March 20, 1939, Wakefield gave Nestlé the right to use her cookie recipe and the Toll House name.

Nestlé offered her $1. Yes, **one dollar**! In trade, rumor has it, Wakefield would receive free Nestlé chocolate for life!

CHOCOLATE BAR SALES

BOARD ROOM

Cookie Detective Query

What made the chocolate chip cookie and Wakefield so interesting to Nestlé?

_____

_____

_____

What do you think of the deal that Nestlé offered to Ruth Wakefield? _____

_____

What deal would you have made? Why? _____

_____

SO YOU SEE,

the journey leading to the

CHOCOLATE CHIP COOKIE

had many twists and turns
over many thousands of years

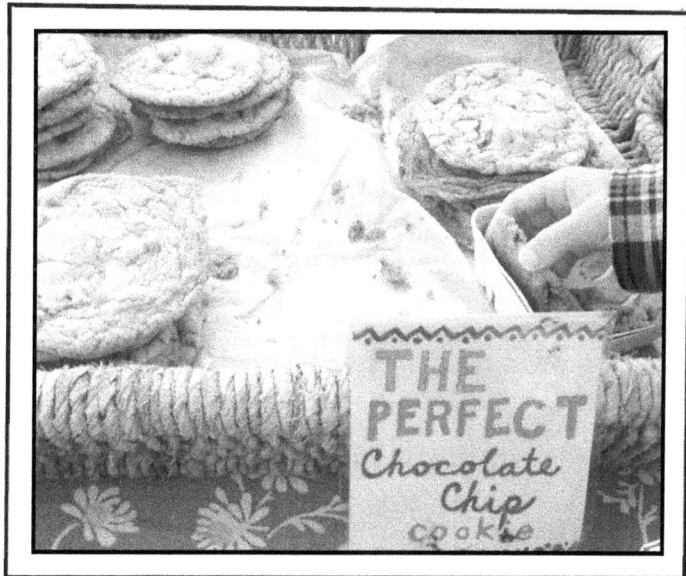

...before landing in your hand!

Now it's time for
YOUR PART IN THIS
EPIC JOURNEY!

PART 2: MAKE COOKIE HISTORY

Time to go from Cookie Detective to Cookie Entrepreneur!

"The important thing is not being afraid to take a chance. Remember, the greatest failure is to not try. Once you find something you love to do, be the best at doing it."

-Debbi Fields, Mrs. Fields Cookies

INTRODUCING LIFE
AS AN ENTREPRENEUR

Your cookie project will teach you many skills people use to start real businesses! Here's a little introduction to business concepts to get you started.

What's an entrepreneur?

The word entrepreneur (en-tre-pre-neur) describes someone who starts a business. Calling people "entrepreneurial" is usually a compliment, saying they are good at starting new businesses.

Entrepreneurs may imagine the business staying small and local, like a small bakery or a local clay-painting studio. Or, they might want a business to get huge, like fast food restaurants or Apple Computer. One of the most famous entrepreneurs was Steve Jobs, who started Apple.

Why start a business?

☐ Freedom in time and flexibility.

☐ Unlimited money potential!

☐ Pursue your own vision for what you want to create. Stay small or get big!

☐ The thrill of solving a problem.

Why NOT do it?

Write down the disadvantages that running your own business might have.

_____

_____

_____

_____

Entrepreneurs use
DETECTIVE SKILLS
to connect the dots to success:

1. Strategize:
Every good project starts with a plan, called a strategy.

2. Deconstruct:
Trace back how successful companies did it and analyze your own results, step by step.

3. Research:
Ask good questions about what your future customers need.

4. Take action:
Plan (tracing forward) using a bit of math, creative thinking, risk taking and team work.

5. Adjust:
Being open to accepting and learning from feedback the is real secret to success. (Testing ideas and "failing fast" is a positive thing in the tech world these days!)

Success Tip
When Thomas Edison was inventing the light bulb, he said, "I have not failed. I've just found 10,000 ways that don't work."

SBA Did you know?

IRL (In Real Life) you can get lots of help from SBA.gov (U.S. Small Business Administration) when starting a small business. Why? Because small businesses create the most jobs in the United States!

TALES OF TWO FAMOUS
COOKIE BUSINESS PEOPLE

Bakeries have existed for hundreds of years. But bakeries that only make cookies are a fairly new idea. Many cookie companies popped up in the 1970s, just like cupcake bakeries did in the 2000s.

Learn about two cookie business pioneers:

Famous Amos

Wally Amos wasn't famous, but he had a great job, working as a talent agent in Hollywood with entertainers. He had a big idea when his job was not going so well. He decided to sell the cookies that his clients loved so much. He set up a cookie bakery in a tiny building on the famous Sunset Strip in Hollywood, California.

His own name made the perfect company name, because it was all about his recipe for crunchy, small cookies by the bagful. People loved his cookies. They quickly became famous!

Eventually the Kellogg Company bought Famous Amos® and turned his fresh baked-cookies into a packaged cookie brand. His big regret about this deal was that he wasn't allowed to use his own name (Wally Amos) to start another cookie business.

Wally Amos moved to Hawaii and kept baking cookies. He decided to focus on helping kids learn to love reading. He also inspires entrepreneurs by speaking and writing about his experiences with his cookie companies and life.

Mrs. Fields Cookies

Debbi Fields started selling her chocolate chip cookies at the age of 13! She used the money she made at another job to buy ingredients. In college, she realized she wanted to do something big and something she loved. She opened a cookie bakery in Palo Alto, California, in the late 1970s. It was the perfect place: a wealthy, college town.

Her own name made the perfect company name, because it was all about her recipe for big, chewy cookies. Her reputation for cookies "baked within the last hour" grew. Her chain of stores grew too!

Eventually an investment firm bought the company and added packaged cookies. This change lined up with her desire to spread her cookies everywhere. Starting in 1990, the stores became franchised. This means anyone can become the owner of a Mrs. Fields® cookie shop.

Debbi Fields now inspires entrepreneurs by speaking about her experiences in starting a successful business. Her stories remind people how important it is to enjoy and learn from both the UPs and the DOWNs of starting a business.

COMPARE
THE COOKIE COMPANIES

Compare and contrast the two stories.

Add what's similar about their stories in the **both** part of this Venn diagram.

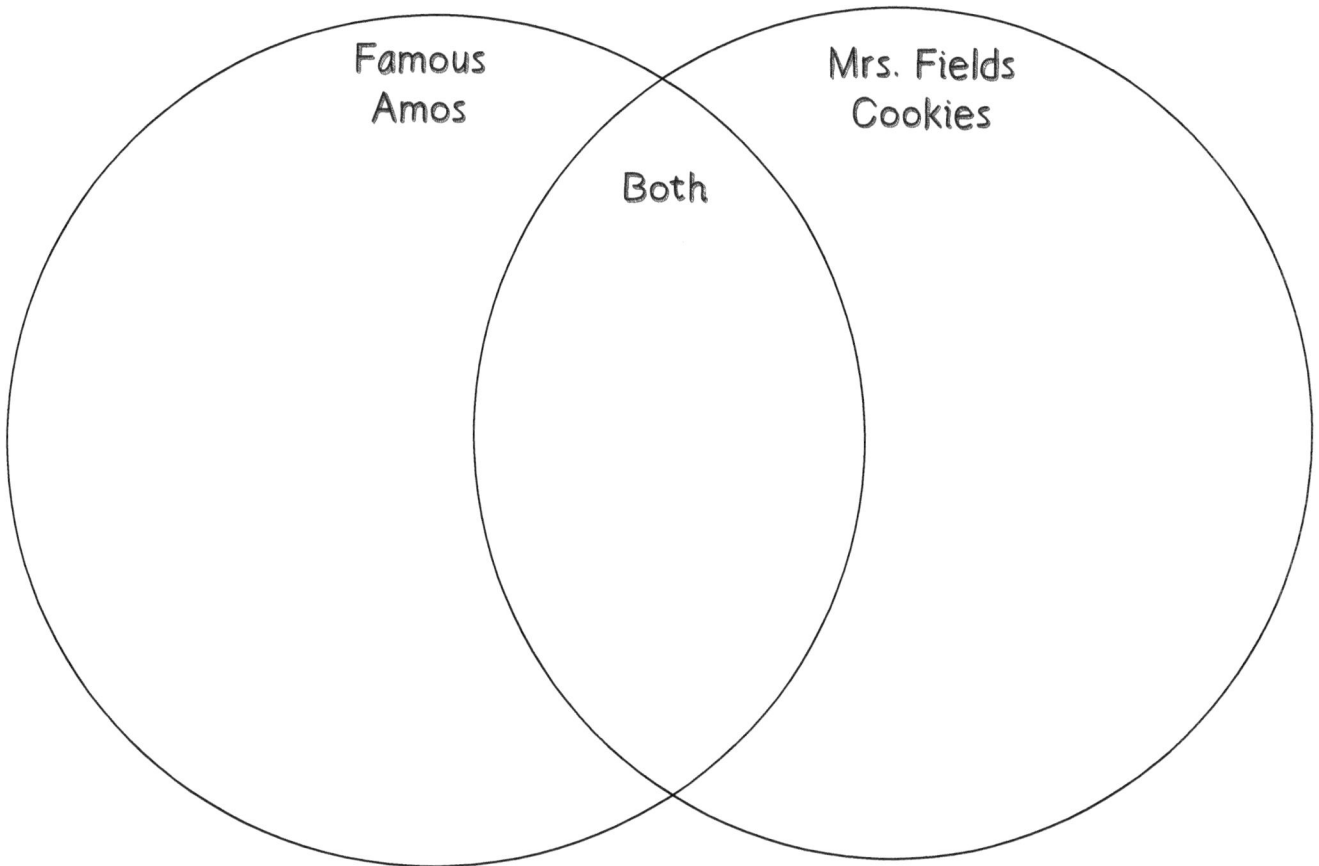

Famous
Amos

Mrs. Fields
Cookies

Both

Cookie Entrepreneur Query

Why do you suppose these stories
of two completely different cookie
companies have so much in common?

_____

_____

_____

_____

What are you curious to know more about?

_____

_____

_____

_____

MEET SOME KIDS ON A MISSION!

See how some kids used food to raise funds for a cause.

MR. CORY'S COOKIES

In 2009, 9-year old "Mr. Cory" was tired of taking the bus to school. He wanted to buy his mom a car. He crafted the idea to sell hot cocoa to raise the funds.

Mr. Cory's mother encouraged him to keep selling hot cocoa to save money for college. He began selling lemonade and cookies to expand options for his loyal customers. Mr. Cory and his mother spent months learning how to bake cookies and test recipes. Mr. Cory's new, natural, homemade chocolate chip cookies were an instant hit.

His impact

Mr. Cory's success comes not only from his delicious treats, but from his very positive attitude, big imagination and drive to succeed. Mr. Cory dreams of making the world better for everyone he knows.

ALEX'S LEMONADE STAND FOUNDATION (ALSF)

Alex (Alexandra) was diagnosed with cancer when she was one year old. When she was four, she opened a lemonade stand with her brother to raise money to help fight cancer.

Her impact

They raised $2,000 and decided to raise funds annually. Alex and her family have been on TV and made several other awareness campaign stops. Alex died when she was eight, and her family continued her foundation.

So far they have raised and donated more than $100 million to support research and programs to fight cancer. Now anyone can "make a stand" against childhood cancer! The guide to raising funds with a lemonade stand is at alexslemonade.org

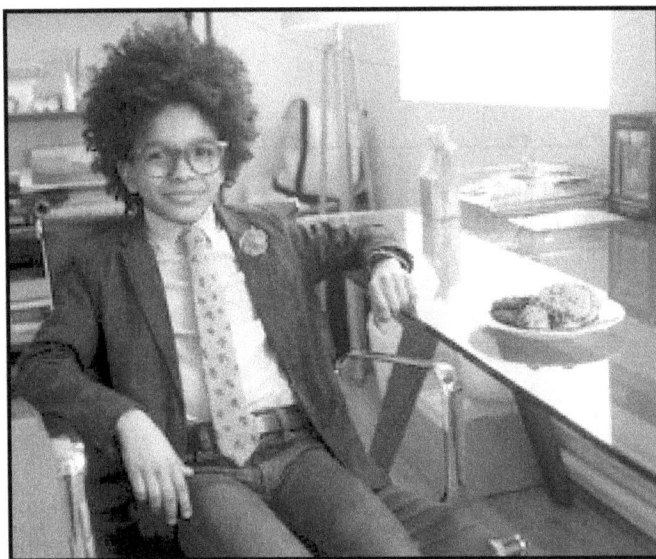

Alex's Lemonade Stand

HELP KIDS WITH CANCER

HOLD YOUR STAND

NOT HORSING AROUND

Lizzie Marie Likness wanted to take horseback riding lessons when she was 6. She told her parents that she would pay for part of the cost. To do so, she started selling healthy homemade baked goods at the local farmer's market.

A couple of years later, she became a spokesperson for the American Heart Association®, and she stars in her own TV show, "Healthy Cooking with Lizzie."

Her impact

Besides baking, she started to teach kids how to have fun cooking healthy meals and living a healthy life. Lizzie says that "the greatest reward is doing what you love for the good of others."

Cookie Entrepreneur Query

What's an example of a company or nonprofit that create good with their cookie sales? How do they do it?

_____

_____

_____

_____

_____

_____

_____

_____

What's a cause you might like help by raising money? Write what you imagine will be your own cookie business success story. It can be unbelievable, inspirational, or just plain plain. Use your wildest imagination of who you're selling to and how big (or small) the company stays. It's your own story!

_____

_____

_____

_____

_____

_____

_____

_____

_____

_____

_____

_____

STEPS TO PLAN
A COOKIE BUSINESS

You already have a ton of knowledge to plan a cookie business!

The next few pages lead you through the steps to plan a real-life business or bake sale, or embark on a fun school project.

OVERVIEW

1. Form your team – You can definitely go it alone, as many cookie entrepreneurs have. When teaming up, you'll make decisions together. That's why knowing who you'll collaborate with is step #1.

2. Research what's out there – Your cookie detective research expedition will give you great ideas and figure out what you want your cookie business to look like.

3. Decide who your customer will be – Having a picture in your mind of who will buy your cookies works wonders. These customers are also called a "target market".

4. Brand it – What makes your cookies and company different? You'll learn how companies get customers!

5. Decide your recipe – Knowing #3 and #4 will help you figure out what your cookies will be like.

6. Get your ingredients – Time to go shopping and do a little cookie math to figure out costs and pricing.

7. Get your tools – You can't bake without a cookie tray! Here you'll learn about the tools to mix, make, serve and store your goodies.

8. Make your cookies – That's right. Cookie time!

9. Promote and sell or give them – BUT before baking the cookies, plan to plan what you'll do with them.

10. Analyze, adjust, repeat – A big part of entrepreneurship is experimentation. You'll take the feedback and ideas you get from your first cookie batch. Then try again or apply your learning to other projects!

STEP 1:
FORM YOUR TEAM

(You may be a team of 1!)

Doing stuff alone is easy. You don't have to coordinate with anyone. No one says you're wrong. There's no one to say "hurry up!" or nag you to slow down. But...there's nothing like a team to make big things happen AND to share the ups and the downs with.

Sometimes, instead of employees, companies hire contractors or agencies for certain roles. However, they're still all one, big, happy team—hopefully!

Learn about the roles in a bakery

The owners of the company are responsible for the success of a business. They need to hire the right people and make customers happy!

The baker may be the company owner, in a new company. Bakers understand the art and science of a great recipe. They come up with recipes, choose the equipment, ingredients and the packaging (boxes, labels and bags). They decide and choose the best ingredients suppliers and equipment for the bakery.

Production staff take over the day-to-day responsibilities as the bakery grows and needs more help. Along with having baking skills, the staff clean, and they help keep the bakery cases full of baked goods.

Sales people may sell to retail stores, like supermarkets, restaurants, cafes and schools. These buyers mark up the price that shopper pays. Why? So they can make money! Bakery sales people call potential buyers at the stores. They make a case for why your cookies are so great. In a small bakery, the baker usually does the sales job.

Marketing team members use their creative and strategic thinking to promote the bakery. They handle advertising, email newsletters, social media, online sales, media relations (for news stories), events and promotions. They are in charge of the company's brand and image, too.

Food scientists are more often found in big baking companies making the kind of packaged cookies you find on supermarket shelves or the freezer section. Food scientists use chemistry skills to figure out exactly how to make the foods. They need to figure out the perfect recipe that fits with a company's goals for shelf life, flavor, price and lots of other qualities. When a bakery is small, the baker does all of this!

Administration team members keep the business running and handle important stuff like hiring, payroll, paying bills, managing computer systems and all the day-to-day workings of a business.

Customer service team members take orders by phone, handle customer feedback and may make deliveries in the beginning, too.

These are just a few of the people that get a small food business, like a bakery, started and growing!

Did you know?

Some states let you run a real bakery at home!

Today nearly all 50 states allow running a small baking business from your home kitchen, to sell locally. This is usually called a "cottage food" or "home-based bakery" business.

What's nice: You won't have to go very far to start baking! And you don't have the added expense of a rental kitchen.

What's not nice: You're limited by the size of your home kitchen and where you can sell. There are also strict rules about pets being in the kitchen. Why do you suppose this is?

Bakers selling fresh bread and pastries usually come to work in the middle of the night.

That's how bakeries can serve early bird customers in the morning. Cookie bakers are lucky. People usually wait until lunch time to start munching. Usually.

Time for Team Cookie!

Maybe you are a team of one. In that case, you'll have fun **wearing many hats** as you plan! If there are a few of you or this is a class project, try picking different roles to see what a real company is like.

How to choose a role?

Just like you'll figure out a career in real life, try this:

- Imagine yourself in the role. What would you be doing? Who would you be interacting with?
- What is the perfect fit for your personality?
- How about choosing a role that is opposite of what is easy? Challenges are a great way to learn!

STEP 2: RESEARCH WITH
COOKIE DETECTIVE WORK

Just like a detective tracks down clues, entrepreneurs need to do research to see what's out there...and what's not.

STEP 1: Get cookie business ideas with a fun "Cookie Research Expedition."

What's a new chocolate chip cookie business idea? Go to the store, or go online, to find out. You'll find lots of packaged cookies, ready-to-bake fresh and frozen dough as well as cookie bakeries.

Choose a few brands to use in your analysis. You don't need to buy them—but if you have some money (and permission) to shop, try this:

- ☐ Start with a budget, like $5 or $10. Try to buy the most packages possible within that budget!
- ☐ Shop smart by comparing the number of cookies and price before buying. Tip: Store shelves often have a price per ounce so you can quickly compare prices.
- ☐ Team up with friends to buy a few brands to share with each other. The goal is to maximize the number of cookies you can analyze...and TASTE!

STEP 2: Analyze the evidence.

Jot down observations about the various cookies. Track your notes using the handy dandy worksheet on the next page, or your favorite way of taking notes.

What to look for:
- ☐ Write down the brand names (which are the company name and cookie names).
- ☐ What are the names like?
- ☐ Who are the packages for — grownups or kids? For on-the-go or eating at home?
- ☐ What's the main thing about the package that makes the cookies interesting? (This is the main, unique benefit that makes a product different from others.)

- ☐ How much do they cost per serving?
- ☐ How much does that break down to cost per cookie?
- ☐ Does this kind of cookie look like one you'd want to buy? Why or why not?

Analyze the ingredients:
- Find the ingredients that don't appear in the classic recipe (on page 6).
- Why might the companies use those ingredients?
- What else do you notice?

Hey, you awesome entrepreneur, circle and fill in the skills needed for research:

observing	comparing	paying attention to detail
reading	making decisions	critical thinking
analyzing	collaborating	

What other skills might come in handy?

_____

_____

_____

_____

_____

_____

COOKIE DETECTIVE RESEARCH WORKSHEET

Cookie brand 1
Company name

Cookie brand name

Who's it for?

_____   _____   _____

The main benefit (why buy?)

_____

Cost per serving

Cost per cookie

Where sold?

_____   _____   _____

Interesting or strange ingredients: _____

Conclusion: _____

Cookie brand 2
Company name

Cookie brand name

Who's it for?

_____   _____   _____

The main benefit (why buy?)

_____

Cost per serving

Cost per cookie

Where sold?

_____   _____   _____

Interesting or strange ingredients: _____

Conclusion: _____

Cookie brand 3
Company name

Cookie brand name

Who's it for?

_____   _____   _____

The main benefit (why buy?)

_____

Cost per serving

Cost per cookie

Where sold?

_____   _____   _____

Interesting or strange ingredients: _____

Conclusion: _____

STEP 3: FIND YOUR
IDEAL CUSTOMER

Some companies make foods then wait for buyers. The most successful companies start with a certain customer in mind, THEN design what their customers want. This is called "design thinking."

This process is what great electronics, game and toy designers do...and why we love their work so much!

WHO will buy your cookies?

_____

_____

_____

If you answered "I don't know!!" that's only natural. You probably noticed the cookies you saw in stores, or online, might appeal to different customers.

WHAT will your cookies be like?

Start by empathizing with your customers. What do your customers really want in a chocolate chip cookie?

The ingredients: Do they have dietary or allergy restrictions? Do they want organic?

_____

_____

The flavor: _____

The size: _____

Chewy, crunchy, etc.? _____

_____

HOW MUCH will they spend on a cookie?

Is the cookie rare and a luxury? Or will you make a lot...so they can be cheaper? _____

_____

WHEN will they buy them? Are they seasonal or all

year long? _____

_____

WHERE do they want to buy them? _____

_____

_____

Cookie Entrepreneur Query

How can you find out about your customers and what they want?

_____

_____

_____

Notice as you go through your day what products or foods you are using. A pen, a notebook, the food you eat, etc. Why are these things just right for you...or not? If you don't like them, who is their ideal customer?

SPECIAL ANNOUNCEMENT TO COOKIE ENTREPRENEURS:

You're about to learn the secret behind ALL THE STUFF YOU BUY. Unlocking this secret will make you A MORE CLEVER SHOPPER and you will use your knowledge when planning YOUR COMPANY.

That secret is all about BRANDING.

"I WANT THE NEW..."

If you've ever said those words, you know the power of a brand.

Brands are unique identities.

It's everything that you think of when you think about a company name or product name. "Nestlé®" is the brand that makes **Toll House® Chocolate Chip Morsels.** The name of those morsels (that most of us call "chips") is a brand name, too.

Quick, what's your favorite cereal? If you thought of oatmeal, well that's a description. If you thought of Quaker® Instant Oatmeal, you thought of a brand.

You know shoe companies, fast food burger places, sports equipment, bike or cell phone maker, apps and even sports teams all because of their unique brands.

Brands include a product's design and packaging.

The shape of a cereal or cookie is part of the overall product design. A company may try to legally protect the design by registering a trademark or design patent. By protecting the design, they can sue copycats and counterfeiters to stop them from making fake versions.

Brands represent a promise to the buyer.

You keep choosing brands you love because of their quality. Or maybe you feel "cool" using that brand. Some brands are popular because they give some of the company's profits to a good cause.

THE BIG GOAL

Businesses all try to create memorable brands that customers love. Happy customers will spread the word about your brand, so your business will grow!

DRAW SOME CONCLUSIONS

Rather, draw some cookies you've seen, then draw conclusions!

Cookie brand:

Cookie brand:

What does the person who buys this kind of cookie WANT?

_____

_____

_____

What does the person who buys this kind of cookie WANT?

_____

_____

_____

Now guess (or ask) what MOTIVATES the buyer to want what they want.

You can try to make this easier by pretending you're the buyer!

The Case of the Missing Chips (Or were they?)

Long ago, Nabisco®, the company who made Chips Ahoy!® Cookies, advertised that each cookie bag had more than 1,000 chips. Well, in 1997 a teacher assigned her students to count the number of chips in a bag. The kids counted fewer than 1,000 chips! How could that be!? Nabisco sent someone from the company to the school. With a little detective work, the company found the kids had not counted the chips that were inside the cookies. It turned out the cookies in the Chips Ahoy! package had a lot more than 1,000 chips, after all.

Your lesson: The design of a cookie, food, or any product needs to be what you tell customers it will be. You never know what kind of detective work they may do to find a flaw! (Bonus lesson: If you do make a mistake, simply be honest and admit it. Customers love honesty, just like friends do.)

PACKAGING POSSIBILITIES

There are so many ways to make and package cookies.

Cookie Critical Thinking Quiz!

A. What makes packaged foods like cookies so popular?

B. Name 5 ways companies try to make cookies inside a package exactly the same.

C. Why do snacks in a package often look exactly the same? (Potato chips were the big exception—until Pringles!)

Resist! Resist reading the answers till you've thought or chatted about the questions!

A. Compared to fresh and custom-made foods (like in a restaurant or bakery), packaged foods cost less and last longer.

B. They'll always have the same width, amount of stuff like chips in the cookie, flavor and thickness.

C. They're easier to produce, predictable to price and package, and customers know what to expect. And that's not all!

Beyond the freshly baked cookies cookies come...

1. packaged for bakery shelves

2. packaged for grocery shelves

3. as dry mix

4. as frozen dough

What are one or more benefits of each type of cookie and packaging? _____

_____

_____

_____

Re-mix one of these packaging ideas and sketch a new design you think is a good idea:

STEP 4: BRAND YOUR COMPANY
WHAT'S IT CALLED?

Chew On This!

The brand name is the name of the company who makes a product. Names don't need to make sense. HARIBO, the company that makes gummi bears and other gummis, combined the first 2 letters of the founder's name and his city: Hans Riegel, Bonn (a city in Germany) = _____ !

Analyze the cookie brands from your Cookie Research Expedition (page 48). What brand names do you love, and why?

_____

_____

_____

_____

_____

Individually come up with 5 names you think might appeal to your target customer.

1._____

2._____

3._____

4._____

5._____

Cookie Critical Thinking

Get in a group of 2-4 (if you've got a group with you, that is).

☐ Think or talk about what your favorite brands make you think about.

☐ Share your 5 name ideas to get feedback. **Remember, there are no bad ideas! Just ideas.**

Get Customer Feedback

Test it out: Ask a couple of people what they think of the name.

Why: This is really useful in case they know that another company has the same name. In real life, you would do a trademark search to confirm the company name is available.

What if they don't like it? It's up to you whether to go for it or change the name. Who ever thought "Amazon" would be an online bookstore?

Cookie Entrepreneur Query

WHAT DOES IT LOOK LIKE?

Making a logo is a good place to start. Your logo can be anything from a simple word typed out to a drawing, either with words or by itself.

The drawing is often called a "brand mark" as it literally marks the brand you think of when you see a symbol and certain colors. Big brands like Ford®, Coca Cola® and Apple® have spent many millions on their logo designs just so you would know the name that goes with their brand mark.

Cookie Entrepreneur Task

Grab a piece of paper or your notebook and start sketching out logo and color ideas.

Even if you have access to a computer, try paper and pencil first – many people find starting with paper makes it easier to be really creative.

Team collaboration rules

- Laugh and have fun with each other's ideas. BUT do not make fun of any ideas. Those could be the winners!
- Build off of each other's ideas.
- Write down or sketch every logo idea, without judging.
- Stay focused on the topic of branding the company.

Logos for thought

What would you expect a brand with logos like these to be like? Who is their customer? Would a logo's color change your mind?

chipperdees

Chipperdees

Chipperdees

chipperdees

CHIPPERDEES

Chipperdees

Planning Shortcut: Make a Flyer!

Making a flyer is a fun way to figure out a LOT about your cookie business, especially if you or your group has creative team members.

Exercise: Try making a flyer on a piece of paper. You will see what details you still need to figure out before you start selling.

Chipperdees

Super Chippy Chocolate Chip Cookies!

Made fresh daily with the BEST ingredients
by Lucy, Adam and Bethany

BAKE SALE FUNDRAISER FOR OUR SOCCER TEAM

Help us meet our $500 GOOOOOAL!

September 3, 11:00-3:00 at the school fair.

Flavor options	# of cookies	Price
Nut free, small	6	$ 3
Nut free, large	12	$ 5.50
Walnuts, small	6	$ 4
Walnuts, large	12	$ 7
Milk chips, small	6	$ 4
Milk chips, large	12	$ 7

BUY 3 BAGS, GET 1 FREE!

The perfect gift! Gift ribbon add $1, gift tin add $5

Also available in bulk for parties.

Email: cookies@chipperdees.com | Text: 555-555-5555 | chipperdees.com

Company name, logo and slogan

Special announcement and incentive

Why buy?

Product options

Incentive to buy more and give them as a gift...and even more!

Contact info

STEP 4: BRAND YOUR COMPANY
PICK YOUR PACKAGING

Keep 3 things in mind when deciding what packaging to use for your cookies:

1. **The usage:** Will customers eat them now or later? Are they gifts? (You thought about this in Step 3.)
2. **Packaging also needs to fit with your brand:** Cutesy? Super simple? Old fashioned?
3. **Your budget:** How much will customers pay, and how much does the packaging cost you?

A few low-cost packaging ideas

- Crinkly cellophane bags
- Paper bags
- Roll top paper bags with a wire closure
- Cardboard boxes
- Metal tins
- Plastic trays / containers
- Sandwich bags (very casual!)
- Shrink wrapped, per cookie
- Glass jars
- Or _____

Figure out your packaging

Shelf life: What's the longest your cookies need to last?

_____

_____

_____

Cost: Gift packaging might cost more than the cookies themselves! Are there "green" options that are recyclable or reusable that you could use?

_____

_____

Cookies in cellophane

Test it out: Ask a couple of people what they think of your packaging idea. In real life, this is important especially when selling to stores. They might want a fancier package or different jar. Or maybe the cookies will crumble.

They don't like it? Using packaging customers like is really important. It's also important that you can make a profit with the packaging that customers like. So be sure to check your cookie budget if you change packaging!

MAKE THE RIGHT COOKIES

Start by choosing the recipe you will use. This step will lead you to then figure out your cookie costs. Below are two GREAT recipes.

Classic Toll House® Cookie Recipe
(This is the one on the chip bags.)

2 1/4 cups all-purpose flour, preferably "unbleached"

1 teaspoon baking soda

1 teaspoon salt

1 cup (2 sticks) butter, softened

3/4 cup granulated white sugar

3/4 cup brown sugar, light or dark

1 teaspoon vanilla extract

2 large eggs

2 cups (12-oz. pkg.) chocolate chips

1 cup chopped walnuts (optional)

Directions

If you have time, refrigerate the batter for 2 or more hours so the ingredients can blend together. **PREHEAT** the oven to 375°F when you're ready to bake. **MAKE** the cookie batter: **STIR** together flour, baking soda and salt in a small bowl. Use a wooden spoon or electric mixer. **BEAT** softened butter, granulated sugar, brown sugar and vanilla extract in a large mixer bowl until creamy. **CRACK THEN ADD** eggs, one at a time, beating well after each addition. **STIR** in flour mixture gradually until the flour is blended in. **STIR** in chips and nuts (if you are using nuts). **DROP** by rounded tablespoon onto ungreased metal baking sheets. **BAKE** for 9 to 11 minutes or until golden brown. **COOL** on baking sheets for 2 minutes. Then use a spatula to move the cookies to wire racks to cool completely.

A Chewy Cookie Twist*
(from Sunset Magazine)

2 cups all-purpose flour, preferably "unbleached"

½ cup quick cooking oatmeal

1 teaspoon baking soda

1 teaspoon salt

1 cup (2 sticks) butter, softened

1-½ cup brown sugar, light or dark.

1 teaspoon vanilla extract

2 large eggs

2 cups (12-oz. pkg.) chocolate chips

1 cup chopped walnuts (optional)

Directions

Make cookie dough using the previous recipe's instructions.

BAKE at 400°F and remove when the centers are still slightly under-done looking. The cookies will keep baking and get really chewy because of all the brown sugar.

> What's the difference between these two recipes?
>
> _____
>
> _____
>
> _____
>
> Circle the verbs that are new to you and find out what they mean.

THE FOLLOWING PAGES HAVE DETAILED TIPS FOR WHEN YOU'RE READY TO BAKE!
Keep on reading to learn a lot more about cookie baking.

You can get creative with chips and other mix-ins.
In your local store, you might find chips in a bunch of flavors like....

Super cookie chips

Butterscotch chips

Milk chocolate chips

Peanut butter chips

Bittersweet chips

Semi-sweet chocolate chips

Along with Nestlé, old-time American companies like Ghirardelli Chocolate, Guittard Chocolate, Hershey Chocolate sell lots of the chips for the millions of cookies made each year.

You can get really creative with tiny recipe changes too!

A whole lot of cookbooks and websites claim to know the **perfect** chocolate chip cookie recipe.*

A fun e-book to learn all about cookie chemistry is Tessa Arias' Ultimate Guide to Chocolate Chip Cookies. You can find it at: www.tinyurl.com/makecccookies

You can also try DIY! Experimenting yourself is the ultimate science test...and the ultimate test of your resilience as a cookie entrepreneur.

Get chemistry tips on page 63 and log your results on page 68.

*You know by now that "perfect" means different things to different people.

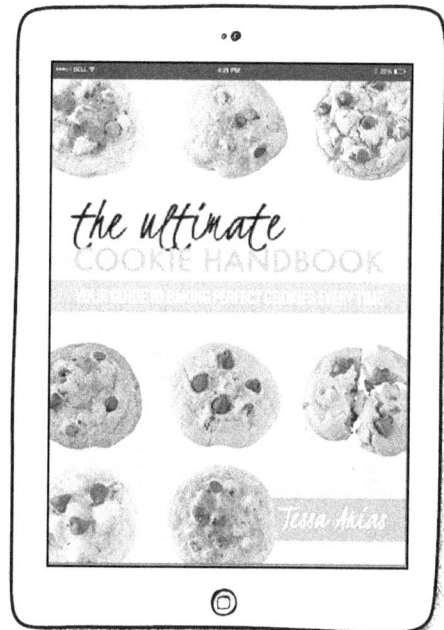

STEP 6: GET YOUR INGREDIENTS
FIRST, DO COOKIE MATH

Once you've picked a recipe, it's time to get your ingredients. Know all you can about your ingredients, because different brands might make cookies turn out differently! Remember that flour tip about the wheat?

SHOPPING TIPS: Larger package sizes are usually cheaper, because there is less packaging per ounce of food. (Look at the tag on the supermarket shelf to see per-ounce prices.) Remember, you can share a big package with friends or keep leftovers stored safely for later.

Fill in the weight or size of the package you buy.

Calculate your costs

	butter	brown sugar	white sugar	eggs	bottle vanilla	baking soda	flour	salt	chips
Price per package									
% of package used per batch									
$ cost per batch		+	+	+	+	+	+	+	+

Add up the cost per batch to get the total cost per batch: $ _____

How much should each cookie cost?

It's up to YOU! Depends how many cookies you make from each batch. This all goes back to knowing what your customers will pay and what size cookies will be. The power is in your hands to decide!

In Real Life...

Bakeries also need to cover costs of packaging, any charity donations, production space, salaries and a lot more.

Figure out the cost per cookie, at different cookie sizes:

Cost per batch $ _____ ÷ # of cookies per batch _____ = cost per cookie $

Cost per batch $ _____ ÷ # of cookies per batch _____ = cost per cookie $

Cost per batch $ _____ ÷ # of cookies per batch _____ = cost per cookie $

Parents / Teachers: Free online spreadsheet on www.chocolatechipcookieschool.com

STEP 7: GET YOUR TOOLS
HERE'S WHAT YOU'LL NEED

Can't get some of these? Work your skills as an awesome collaborator: Ask friends or neighbors to borrow or share. Or find a similar substitute tool. It's all in the spirit of experimentation!

Mixing bowl — This can be any clean bowl, the size for a big salad or popcorn.

Measuring cups — **Dry measuring cups** are for flour and white sugar. To measure accurately, use a flat tool, like the back of a knife, to flatten the top, pushing off any extra. Pack **brown sugar** in tightly like wet sand!

Measuring spoons — Flatten baking soda and other ingredients across measuring spoons.

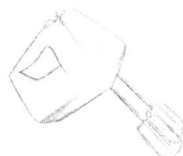

Electric mixer — Some people use a hand-held mixer or a stand mixer (like a KitchenAid™). If you want some exercise, a big spoon works too!

Mixing spoon — Wooden spoons are great but any big spoon will work.

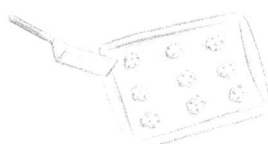

Baking sheet or "sheet pan" — The bigger the metal baking sheet, the faster your cookie production goes. Some sheets have are designed to let air flow, to prevent your cookies from burning on the bottom.

Potholder — You didn't need to be told you can't grab a hot pan with your hand, right? Use a thick potholder or folded towel. Ask an adult to help.

Oven — The oven needs to be large enough to fit the cookie sheet, and the oven temperature needs to be accurate. If it's not, look at any cookie catastrophes as a learning experience!

Cooling rack — Cooling racks let air flow around the cookies as they cool down. (It's ok if you don't have one of these though.)

Storage container — Keep the cool cookies air-tight to stay fresher longer.

Serving plate — Choose a plate that will show off your cookies, either a big one or small with the cookies piled up.

STEP 8: MAKE YOUR COOKIES
COOKIE MAKING DETAILS

Here are some tips for how to handle the ingredients if you are new to baking. Log your exact steps and results, in case you want to do something different next time.

STEP 1: Blend the "wet" mixture in a big bowl.

1. Measure the brown sugar, packing it as tightly into the measuring cups as you can. It should be level, not in a dome shape. Dump it into the mixing bowl.

2. Measure the white sugar, leveling the top of the measuring cup with a knife or wooden spoon handle.

3. Add the butter, and stir it with the sugar.

4. Crack the 2 eggs into the bowl by tapping the middle on the edge of the bowl. Stick one finger into the cracked egg shell to pull it apart. Then wash your hands with soap. Pieces of egg shell in the mix? Simply pick it out. Wash again!

5. Add the vanilla extract. Stir until blended and creamy.

STEP 2: Mix the "dry" ingredients in another bowl (or the same bowl; just dry it REALLY well first!).

6. Measure the flour, leveling the top of the measuring cup with a knife or wooden spoon handle.

7. Measure the baking soda, flattening it with a dull knife or another flat object.

8. Measure the salt, also making it flat across the measuring spoon.

9. Mix the wet and dry together, just until well blended. As flour mixes with moist ingredients, gluten (a tough network of connected proteins) forms. More beating means tougher baked goods.

10. Mix in chips (and nuts if you like) into the dough.

STEP 3: Make cookies! Put the rack in the oven at the center level. Then preheat oven to the temperature for your recipe.

11. Pinch or scoop dough in desired size. Space the balls a couple of inches apart.

12. Pop the tray in the heated oven, preferably baking one tray at a time. Bake for the amount of time specified in your recipe.

13. Remove the tray using a potholder. Remove the cookies with a spatula, and place them on metal racks to cool or on a plate, if you don't have racks.

14. Analyze the cookies. Did they turn out as planned?

Did you know?

There's an expression measure twice, cut once. That refers to cloth. In the world of cookies you might say: "Measure twice, bake once."

Experiment!

Small changes in time and heat can make a huge difference. So can these tricks:

- Try chilling the dough for a few hours or overnight. This gives the flour more time to soak in liquids like butter and eggs. Many bakers believe this is the secret to the best cookies!

- You might try browning the butter in a pan before using for a more caramelized flavor.

Understanding Chocolate Chip Cookie Chemistry

Cookies In Action

1. As butter warms, the dough spreads & edges get thinner.

2. The edges bake and stop spreading. The higher the temperature, the sooner this will happen.

3. Liquid from butter and eggs dissolve baking soda.

4. Sugar caramelizes as granules melt together.

8. The "Maillard Reaction": Flour and egg proteins and sugar transform with heat to brown and create a nutty flavor.

7. Gases cause cookies to rise.

6. Dough expands, adding crevices.

5. Egg protein and wet starches begin to set.

9. Sugar hardens during cooling for crisp caramel effect.

10. Air cools the cookies and they sink a little.

No raw cookie dough!

It's a bad idea to eat uncooked cookie dough. Even when well-washed, eggs can cause salmonellosis, a type of food poisoning that's really not nice. Hazards can enter the baking process at many points during preparation of cookies. If you're going to have a stomach ache, it should be from eating too many cookies, not from food poisoning!

Fun Fat Facts

Margarine: The moisture in low-fat products may differ from butter, so you may need to adjust the other ingredients.

Butter: Gluten can't form in fat. More butter adds water, which leads to more tender cookies, and the more they will spread when baking. Butter also adds caramel flavor.

Eggs add moisture as they are 73% water, 13% protein, 12% fat.

Fascinating Cookie Chemistry

Amazingly, even one little change when you're cooking or baking can completely change the result! Discuss why each recipe factor can totally change your results:

☐ Measurements
☐ Ingredients brands
☐ Mixing order
☐ Cookie size
☐ Time after mixing but before baking
☐ Type of baking sheet
☐ Temperature and oven accuracy
☐ Placement in oven
☐ Amount of baking time
☐ What else? _____

_____

_____

STEP 9: PROMOTE AND SELL
PREPARE TO THRILL

Your bake sale, or cookie selling event or party is the real test for your cookies and for your business.

Just get it out there & enjoy!

Remember way back on page 4, imagining the first time someone at a chocolate chip cookie? One day, you might look back at the first time someone ate YOUR cookies!

A simple way to get started is to sell for the holidays, summer fun or as after-school sports snacks.

Use the checklist on the right to help you prepare for success.

Bake Sale Checklist

- ☐ Decide your goal for the sale. How much money do you need to make to reach that goal? (See page 42 for ideas from kids' businesses.)
- ☐ Pick a date when a lot of people will be in town.
- ☐ Get packaging for the cookies.
- ☐ Get cookie ingredients and tools. Make plenty of cookies to sell. (Plan to have samples to hand out. Samples sell!)
- ☐ Make signage, and have a way to hang it.
- ☐ Find a cash box and small bills for change and / or another way to take payment (like a smartphone app).
- ☐ Find a busy location for the sale.
- ☐ Print handouts with ordering information.

Preparation
- ☐ Figure out your costs.
- ☐ Price the cookies, maybe with a **buy 5, get 1 free** promotion? (Make sure to include free cookies in your cost calculation!)
- ☐ Bake, bake, bake!
- ☐ Package, package, package!

At the Sale
- ☐ Be enthusiastic!
- ☐ Tell people all about you and product.
- ☐ Let customers know you want them to be satisfied and ask for feedback.

Stay in touch
- ☐ Hand out your contact information.
- ☐ Ask for contact information with a sign-up sheet to promote future sales.

Get a bake sale template you can customize on www.ChocolateChipCookieSchool.com

STEP 10: ANALYZE, ADJUST, REPEAT
BUT FIRST: CELEBRATE!

> Give yourself a HUGE pat on the back for all of your great work!

Now, use your Cookie Detective skills on yourself!

Just like a huddle after a game, huddle over your cookie business results and see what's working and what you'd like to change.

1. Gather the results of your cookie sales.

- ☐ Review any feedback from people who bought cookies.
- ☐ Calculate your profit. Subtract expenses from the money you received.

  Total $ Received - Expenses = Profit

2. Analyze the results of the sale.

- ☐ Did many customers have similar suggestions?
- ☐ Are you happy with how things went?
- ☐ How did the results compare to what you expected?

3. Decide what might want to change next time.

- ☐ Sales lower than expected? You might need to change the price. Or change your customers! Maybe the cookies are perfect, but different promotion will help sell more and reach different people.
- ☐ How might you make more money?
- ☐ What more do you want to learn?
- ☐ How can the overall experience be more fun and interesting for you?

WANT TO GET REAL?
GOOD NEWS - YOU'VE DONE THE WORK THAT GOES INTO PLANNING A BUSINESS!

In real life, if you need help starting a business, the first question you get is: "What's the plan?" A business plan is like a roadmap for a successful business. Here's an outline for how you can organize your cookie project ideas into a plan.

An easy one-page business plan

The business goal
What is the purpose of having the business?

For example: Raise $100,000 for children's business education while creating a profitable business selling delicious, healthy chocolate chip cookies.

Your ideal customer
Who will buy your products, so you can reach the goal?

- Local parents who want to save time with after school snacks
- Local kids who love our cookies and want to support the cause
- Local school cafeterias

Strategies
What you'll do to accomplish the goals.

For example:

- Give 100% of profits* to the charity
- Depend on partners for donations and people who will work for free, for experience and the cause

*after expenses

Tactics for the first year
Specific tasks to achieve those strategies

For example:

- Partner with 10 charities for social media
- Create packaged cookies kids can sell for after school sports teams
- Involve food purchasing managers as part of the team
- Ask local supermarkets to donate ingredients

Success measurement
How will you know when the business is a success?

For example:

- $100,000 profit by December 31
- Promotion in local newspapers
- 2,000 social media followers

This is a very simple but real plan outline. Visit www.chocolatechipcookieschool.com for templates you can copy.

CONGRATULATIONS!

_____
(your name)

· ·

You are officially a COOKIE DETECTIVE and ENTREPRENEUR.

· ·

Remember all the cookie history lessons, and keep your curiosity, critical thinking and spirit of adventure growing! That's the secret to creating and getting wonderful things in life.

COOKIE DETECTIVE LOG

A place to take notes, jot thoughts, etc.

Cookie School Notes

COOKIE CRITICAL THINKING
NEXT STEPS

Keep the conversation going at home, school and in the supermarket!

What were the 5 most interesting things you learned? Why?

What are you curious to know more about?

How do the cookie stories and business ideas relate to other foods and products we buy?

What kinds of questions will you ask the next time you have a cookie in your hands?

Here are a few ideas for getting started as an entrepreneur, whether with cookies or something else!

- Set a goal to raise money for a charity, vacation, new computer or college fund.
- Ask your parents and your friends' parents how you might help them raise money or provide cookies for after-school sports snacks or parties.
- Use your knowledge to ask big food companies to change their ingredients.
- Create a product to help growers of certain ingredients (like cacao) earn a better living.

Share what you're up to with the Chocolate Chip Cookie School so we can bring you extra fame!

COMPARE THE COOKIE STORIES

As you saw on page 5, the cookie stories, or legends, fall into a few basic themes. As a Cookie Detective, it's up to YOU to decipher the steps leading to that moment when the cookies were done baking that first time.

> Which could be true?

RUTH GRAVES WAKEFIELD

Can you discover the true story?

1. Think about each of the chocolate chip cookie invention stories, below.

2. Chart the actions and decisions that could have led to the cookie's invention.

3. Decide which story is most likely to be true!

STORY 1: "IT WAS INVENTED ON PURPOSE."

Some say Ruth Graves Wakefield invented the cookie on purpose, either because she ran out of nuts, or because she wanted to create something interesting and different for diners at the Inn.

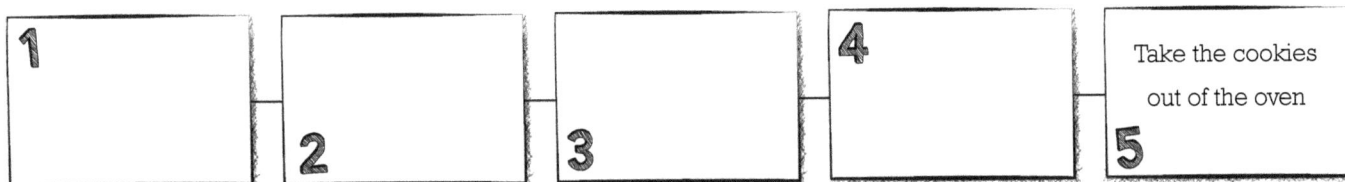

1	2	3	4	5 Take the cookies out of the oven

STORY 2: "IT WAS A FREAK ACCIDENT!"

The Toll House Inn's baker said vibrations caused by their big mixer caused chocolate on a shelf to jiggle over, fall into the mixer while no one was watching, break up into bits and get mixed into the dough.

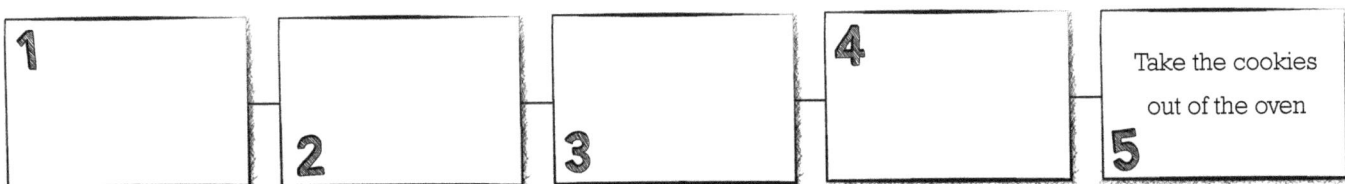

1	2	3	4	5 Take the cookies out of the oven

STORY 3: "THE RECIPE CAME OUT WRONG!"

Some people said Wakefield intended to make a **chocolate** cookie. The chocolate that Wakefield usually used would have melted into the dough, BUT she had run out of this chocolate. The Nestlé chocolate bar that she chopped up did NOT melt. The chocolate stayed in "chip" form—and she decided to serve the cookies anyway.

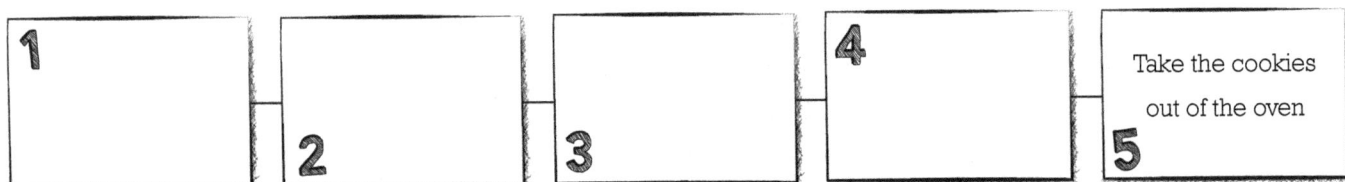

1	2	3	4	5 Take the cookies out of the oven

Which of the 3 stories is most likely to be true? _____

Why do you think that? _____

What questions do you have about each story?

_____

_____

_____

_____

Cookie Detective Query

Discuss! Maybe even re-enact!

— Be the Storyteller! —

See how easily stories spread in different ways.

- ☐ Make up your own version of the chocolate chip cookie invention. You can base it on what you've read. Or make up a completely new story.
- ☐ Test out your stories on friends or classmates. Do they believe them?
- ☐ Optionally, whisper your story to a friend and pass the story through a line of people. Have the last person tell you the story. Has it changed from what you first said?

We've filled in the first few words to help you get started (kind of like starting with a cookie mix).
Feel free to ignore those starter words and start from scratch!

Gossip: Can you believe… _____

Rumors: They say that… _____

Legends: We can't prove it but… _____

Urban legend: A friend of my great grandma said… _____

_____

Tall tales and fables: Once there was… _____

_____

_____

ABOUT THIS BOOK

Genius is 1% inspiration and 99% perspiration.

–Thomas Edison

The Inspiration

When you realize that "making cookies" is what makes you happiest, yet you don't want to start a cookie business, what do you do?

Susie Wyshak was writing a similar book for adults, called **Good Food, Great Business: How to Take Your Artisan Food Idea From Concept to Marketplace**. One daym on an break from writing, she was making cookies with her niece and nephew. They asked lots of questions about the science, geography and history of cookie ingredients. The idea for this book struck! You're reading the result of this inspiration.

The Perspiration

Thanks to many Kickstarter supporters who funded the book, parents and kids providing feedback, creative contributors and educators who offered the chance to test out the cookie concept in elementary schools, you are reading the result of much perspiration!

DOWNLOAD PRINTABLE ACTIVITIES

Kids, parents and teachers, get links to printables and worksheets at
www.ChocolateChipCookieSchool.com

Email: susie@chocolatechipcookieschool.com

FACEBOOK / TWITTER: cccookieschool

THANK YOU
KIND SUPPORTERS!

BIG thank yous to these wonderful supporters and contributors:

M&M, my sisters Jeanne, Patty and Robin, Mom & Dad, Erin Alexander, Xiomara Cotton, Phuongmai Truong, Catherine Graham, Christine Hanson, Tim Holmes & Mitch Huitema, The Huffs, The Woodards, Seng Lovan, Margaret Gilmore, Tim Allen, The Chocolate Chip Sugar Daddy :), Carrie Arul, Gina Guidi, Andy Astor, Frieda de Lackner, Julia Kendrick Conway – Assaggiare Mendocino, Randi Shade, Kimberly Blessing, Jon Øso, Hannah Rosenberg, Todd Masonis, Cynthia Hulton, Isolde Gabrielle Rodriguez de Webb, Deb Mazzaferro, Peter Kelsey, Paul T. Jobson, Heather Dean, FARMcurious, Rafael Ebron, East Bay Co(okie)housing, Lisa Scott and Finn, Heathervescent, David Sperman, Yuan Weigel. Clay Gordon, choconancy, Mia Watson, Jesse Manis, Montse, Gabriela Rodriguez, Shelley Seward, Annie (the) Baker, Cethy, Nahua Chocolate (Costa Rica), Regina Dowling Jones, Maura Sell, Andy Fisher, Mohsin & Tasmia, Jaworski Family, Buyer's Best Friend, Bob Lord, Mindy Fong, Rajkumari Neogy, Peter and Gwen Jacobsen, Clarine Hardesty, Sean Timberlake, Jennie Schacht, Carl Nicolari, Brett Fisher, JoAnn Uhelszki, Molly Curry, Avanthi Kanmatareddy, Lisa G, Mavvy Vasquez, Eric Mueller, Chris Angelli, Deb McClanahan, Kristy Duncan, Luke Anderson, Tracy E. Turner, Natasha Hayes, Frankie Whitman, Catt Fields White, Cindy Friedman, Robert MacKimmie – citybees.com, Sarit Neundorf, Nina Wanat, Amy B Sherman, Emily LaFave, Meesha Halm, @KarlSF, A Little Yumminess, Eat My Words, Mohr Media LLC, Melissa Karam, Daniela Vasquez V., Laurie Young, Nancy E., Corin Goodwin, Anita Chu, Vanessa Barrington, Jame Ervin, Jena Chambers, Leigh Anne Vanhoozer, Rachel Zemser, Vera Devera, Kathy Henderson, Jennifer Lemon, Cristina Rosales, Lisa Golden, Sarah Cornelius, Kim Ruby, Liza Barry-Kessler, Mike Schmitt, Janelle Orsi, Claudius Gayle, Kimberly Hanson, Lenka G., Veronica Pfeil, Lucky Dog Hot Sauce, Elaine Wu, Christopher West, Break Brittle Cashew Brittles, Scott F., Monette Olivera-Pangan, Melanie A. Gabbard, The Chapter Book Academy, Josh/ Mascott Books… and all the anonymous contributors.

Kickstarter Reward Partners

Many thanks to **ECO Lips** for custom-made chocolate chip cookie lip balm and **La Faza** vanilla.
COOKIE ADVENTURE BAKERIES: In California: Berkeley: Pacific Cookie Company and CREAM; Davis: CREAM; Santa Monica: Cookie Good; Napa: Annie the Baker; Oakland: Bittersweet Chocolate Cafe; Palo Alto: CREAM; San Francisco: The Mill; San Jose: CREAM; Santa Cruz: Pacific Cookie Company; Walnut Creek: CREAM;

In Colorado (Denver): Victory Love Cookies; Georgia (Decatur): The Cookie Studio; Massachusetts (Boston): Have a Sweet Idea; Michigan (Ann Arbor): Zingerman's Bakehouse and Tasty Bakery; New York: Levain Bakery; North Carolina (Ashville): French Broad Chocolates; Ohio (Lakewood): Blackbird Baking; Oregon (Portland): Pearl Bakery; Pennsylvania (Philadelphia): Famous 4th St Bakery; South Carolina (Charleston): WildFlour Pastry; Texas (Austin): Sugar Mama's; Washington (Seattle): Macrina Bakery; Wyoming (Jackson): Persephone

REFERENCES & RESOURCES

For links to printable worksheets, articles, more books, recipes, websites used for ingredients research, and stories visit ChocolateChipCookieSchool.com/links

Ingredients Research Websites

HistoryForKids.org

Smithsonian.com

Wikipedia.com (source of many historic photos)

Key Books and Magazine Articles

- ☐ Abbott, Elizabeth, Sugar: A Bittersweet History, London: Duckworth, 2009.
- ☐ Amos, Wally, The Cookie Never Crumbles: Practical Recipes for Everyday Living, New York: St. Martin's Press, 2001.
- ☐ Aronson, Marc and Marina Budhos, Sugar Changed the World: A Story of Magic, Spice, Slavery, Freedom, and Science, New York: Clarion Books, 2010. (Also see: Sugarchangedtheworld.com)
- ☐ Daley, Bill, "Measuring up: Fannie Farmer Shaped the Nation's Appetites, Taught Cooks Precision", Tribune Newspapers: Chicago, March 21, 2012.
- ☐ Farmer, Fannie, The Boston School of Cookery Cookbook, 2nd Ed., Boston: Little, Brown and Company, 1906.
- ☐ Gisslen, Wayne, Professional Baking, Sixth Ed., New Jersey: Wiley, 2012.
- ☐ Kurlansky, Mark, Salt: A World History, New York: Walker Books, 2002.
- ☐ Michaud, Jon, "Sweet Morsels: A History of the Chocolate-Chip Cookie", New Yorker Magazine, December 19, 2013.
- ☐ Mintz, Sidney, Sweetness and Power: The Place of Sugar in Modern History, New York: Penguin Books, 1985.
- ☐ Presilla, Maricel E., The New Taste of Chocolate: A Cultural & Natural History of Cacao With Recipes, Berkeley: Ten Speed Press, 2009.
- ☐ Rain, Patricia, The Vanilla Cookbook: The Cultural History of the World's Favorite Flavor & Fragrance, 2nd Ed., New York: Tarcher, 2004.
- ☐ Wyman, Carolyn, The Great American Chocolate Chip Cookie Book: Scrumptious Recipes & Fabled History From Toll House to Cookie Cake Pie, Woodstock: The Countryman Press, 2013.